The Sky Within
A Memoir of Sleep

BACKLASH
PRESS

A pioneering publishing house dedicated to creating intelligent, vivid books. Established to inform, educate, entertain and provoke.

A Backlash Press Book

First published 2022

backlashpress.com

Book designer: The Scrutineer, Rachael Adams
Illustrations pages 13, 41, 94 & 95: Klaudia Wosik
Chapter heading illustrations: Sarah Dudgeon

Printed and bound by TJ Books Ltd, Padstow, Cornwall, UK

ISBN: 978-1-7391016-0-2

All rights reserved. No part of this publication may be reproduced, stored in a retrieval system or transmitted in any form or by any means, electronic, mechanical, photocopying, recording or otherwise, without permission of the copyright holder.

Copyright © Rebecca Stonehill
The moral rights of the author have been asserted.

Rebecca Stonehill

The Sky Within Rebecca Stonehill

Backlash Poetry

American Dangerous: Renée Olander
Bombing the Thinker: Darren C. Demaree
Burial Machine: Jacob Griffin Hall
Clay Unbreakables: Natalia I Andrievskikh
Into The The: Robin Reagler
Phantom Laundry: Michael Tyrell
Tattered Scrolls and Postulates: Joseph V Milford
The Arsonist's Letters: Michael Tyrell
The Life in the Sky Comes Down: Bruce Bromley
Unfinished Murder Ballads: Darren C. Demaree

Backlash Journals

#1
#2
#3: Provoke
#4
Isolation
#5

For Andy,
for holding me

And for Maya, Lily & Benji,
for accepting me just as I am

The Sky Within Rebecca Stonehill

Contents

Starfish	15
A Story of a Beginning	17
The Story of Thoughts	23
Coeur	29
Gold Dust	43
The Sky Within	49
The Spaciousness of Uncertainty	61
Day and Night Gifts	69
A Lamp to Yourself	79
The End of the Story	89
Acknowledgements	97
Resources and Further Reading	99

The Sky Within Rebecca Stonehill

The Sky Within
Rebecca Stonehill

The Sky Within Rebecca Stonehill

'The heart that breaks open can contain the whole universe.'

Joanna Macy

The Sky Within Rebecca Stonehill

The Sky Within Rebecca Stonehill

Starfish

Wasini Island: a dot in the Indian Ocean, off the Kenyan coast and close to an invisible line flowing into Tanzanian waters. This is a tiny island of mangroves and mosques, of crystal waters populated by pods of playful dolphins and soaring baobab trees.

It is Christmas Eve in 2016 and my family and I have travelled to the coast from our Nairobi suburb where we are living. We are staying in an open-sided, thatched *banda*, a small hut, our electricity powered by the sun and stone water-filled urns in the shade serving as fridges. The morning is spent playing in the natural pool created at high tide that hugs the cliffside. As the day drifts lazily into afternoon, the tide creeps out to create a myriad of rockpools, my three children gasping in delight as they discover starfish and brightly coloured seashells. We choose a few of those shells and hang them from a festive branch in our *banda* and they glimmer like baubles in the sunlight. For dinner, we eat fresh crab and vegetables in coconut milk whilst listening to the distant *muezzin's* call to prayer on the warm evening air.

We have been living in Kenya for three years, moving here from London for my husband's job in water and sanitation for marginalised urban communities. Spending Christmas on a palm-fringed, off-grid island is like a dream come true. It is probably as close to paradise as I will ever come. Not only that, but I have a loving husband and three wonderful, healthy children. I've never known true hunger, I don't have a life-threatening illness and I always go to bed with a roof over my head. What is more, I am living the dream I've harboured for more years than I can remember of being a writer and the gratitude for all these things and more is so intense that it aches beneath my ribcage.

And yet, as I sit at a distance from the *banda* on the clifftop that Christmas Eve, wrapped in the night that dazzles with pinpricks of stars, I don't want to be alive anymore. I hug my knees into my chest and my body is racked with sobs, wave after wave of them that feel like they have no beginning and no end. Looking up, the Indian Ocean is an inky expanse of smooth

The Sky Within Rebecca Stonehill

blackness and I wonder how it would feel to just float away, to be pulled into nature's currents and become one with the vast waters that interlink their watery hands across the surface of the planet.

As my sobbing lessens, I take a deep inhale. Can I really do it? How much do I want it? How much do I crave this oblivion that could put an end to the anguish I feel at the core of my being? Earlier that evening as my husband and I tried to coax our children to sleep, they'd hung their stockings at the end of their beds beneath the mosquito nets. *Does Father Christmas come to Wasini Island?* they'd asked. *Is he the same Father Christmas here or a different one?* Finally, flushed from the sun and exhausted from the excitement of the day, they had lain in their beds as we'd pulled thin cotton sheets over them. I was about to duck back under the mosquito net when I noticed a small folded up piece of paper sticking out of the top of my seven-year-old daughter's stocking. As her eyelids tugged downwards, I picked up the paper and unfolded it.

Dear Father Christmas, it read. *Please can I have some snacks. And please can you bring my Mummy some sleep?*

Exhale.

And rewind.

A Story of a Beginning

Is there ever really a beginning? Or do our stories lie buried in us, coiled up like sleeping snakes waiting to be woken?

The story I always liked to tell myself and other people was that I stopped sleeping well when I was pregnant with my first child. It was a neat narrative, contained in the comfort of a box with the stamp of reason and purpose sealed securely on it. And it worked: people seemed to understand that, nodding their heads and sagely murmuring about hormones and lifestyle changes. Better still, it made me feel normal, because lots of mothers stop sleeping when they are pregnant.

And yet the truth of it, I realise now, is rather harder to unpick. For better or for worse, the writer-in-training in me always kept a diary, ever since the tender age of six. *I never travel without my diary*, says Gwendolyn Fairfax in Oscar Wilde's play The Importance of Being Earnest. *One should always have something sensational to read in the train.* I'm not sure if I ever viewed my diaries as sensational but I do know that, in a hidden corner of my mind, I was writing myself into being. Somehow, in a way that would have been impossible to articulate, I wasn't just writing for myself.

Looking back over my diaries now, I wonder if perhaps it would be a more truthful story to zoom in on the smattering of pages from the age of eight when I lie upstairs in my bed, my fingers pressed into my ears to drown out the sounds downstairs of somebody who is slowly replacing my father? Or how about, at the age of eleven, away for the first time at boarding school in a dormitory room with seven other girls and I am kept awake by snoring from the next bed, eventually bursting into tears and being taken out by an irate housemistress for disturbing the others? Or four years after that, when I am diagnosed with Crohn's Disease and spend weeks on end in hospital on the children's ward, a plastic curtain hastily pulled round my bed, attuned to every sound, every murmur beyond my pocket of 'privacy?'

I was an introverted yet sociable and content child, never happier than when

The Sky Within Rebecca Stonehill

I had my nose in a book and I fervently adored the ritual of primary school, the neat grey pinafore and long socks, Wednesday roller-skating and my circle of friends. I'm sure it provided an anchor for me in a rather less secure homelife which, whilst very far from traumatic, was marked by change. My parents separated when I was five years old, my much older father moving to Switzerland. There was always something abrasive in my relationship with him when he visited us in England or we went out to the mountains to see him; I loved him and his absence ached in some indiscernible part of me, but he felt very far from a father in the traditional sense. When we spent time with him, he often seemed to be working and his age meant that, rather than being a hands-on Dad, he was like an enthusiastic grandfather whom I never knew well enough to open up to. My relationship with my mother was easier to define and I remember her always being there for me and providing the stable backdrop to my younger years. More challenging, however, was coming to terms with her new relationships as she navigated her own loneliness. I was also close to my older brother and younger sister but when my brother was seven, he went to boarding school and, just like that, I lost one of my closest allies, a boy I remember always being beside me in my tender years.

Try as hard as I might to glean clues from the countless scrawls over hundreds of pages in every colour imaginable, the truth is that I will never quite know which of these experiences provided the spark of a beginning of my sleeplessness. Perhaps it is a combination; perhaps it is simply the seismic shift of becoming a mother; or perhaps it is none of these things at all. What I do know, reading back over nine months of diary entries of my first child's pregnancy is that the story I had been spinning for so many years was actually not inaccurate. Because I didn't write about being tired or struggling with sleep. I talked about being uncomfortable, particularly as the months progressed and the occasional night of not being able to find an accommodating position for my growing bump. But exhausted from lack of sleep? No. Quite the opposite in fact; I appear to be dashing about from one hen night to the next, settling into and decorating a new home my husband, Andy, and I bought, cycling myself and my growing bump to a succession of temping jobs and then, when these finish during my last month of pregnancy, growing round and content in the sun. How fickle memory is. The week before I give birth, I write these words in my diary:

I did some yoga as I listened to the bird song from outside and felt the breeze wafting in through the window. And I put my hand on my belly and felt the baby moving around and I thought to myself, there are few moments as beautiful as this one. This is it. This is a new chapter.

Yet the chapter that is to come is not what I am expecting. When my daughter is born, the tone changes, though it's a slow and subtle shift into anything problematic. I start to write about 'deep exhaustion' and feeling 'tearful.' *Nap during the day when your baby sleeps,* everybody suggests. So I try, but the more I 'try', the more impossible that becomes. I am wired, deeply in love with my daughter but in constant fight, flight mode and napping during the day becomes an abstract longing. Even when she begins to sleep well and feeding is long behind me, by this stage, the night has taken on proportions of immensity. I can't switch off. I don't know how to relax anymore.

I go for acupuncture, for *reiki,* for hypnotherapy. I take supplements and join a group CBT class. I visit the GP and they write me a prescription for sleeping pills, advising me to proceed with caution. More often than not, the sleeping pills don't work. I go full circle and try out every natural remedy and treatment I can think of. When none of these give my body and mind the rest I am craving, I return to the GP and I am put on my first of many anti-depressants. I become conversant in the language of NHS depression, marking on a scale of one to ten my state of mind and my willingness to lead a social life. Some treatments and therapies give me temporary relief from the desperation I feel. Some of the anti-depressants, for example, manage to give me several months of a reasonable quality of life. And reasonable is good. Reasonable, as far as I am concerned, is liveable. But then they stop working, just like that, and the fall-out from the crash hits me hard. I begin to feel then, as I have felt many times since, that I am living on one side of a glass wall and life is being lived out on the other side. I can watch, but I can't reach it.

When my child is just over a year old, I write these words in my diary:

*If I could change **one** thing about my life – just one – I would sleep well, or decently each night. When I've slept well, I feel as though I can conquer the world. I have energy, I am sociable, I want to get out and do things, I am chatty. When I don't sleep, I feel as though the world is against me. Like now. It's a miserable feeling.*

Reading this in my diary almost comes as a shock, because I feel that these same words have been written a multitude of times, just couched in slightly different language. Years later, it's not easy to see this painfully similar sentiment glare up at me from the page, my inner critic immediately

The Sky Within Rebecca Stonehill

jumping in to comment that nothing has changed after all these years. Is it helpful to listen to this voice? No. Is it kind? Most definitely not.

I limp along, but it isn't really until my second child is born, two years after my first, that the tone in my diaries take on a dramatic shift, the opposing extremes of desperation ('I am struggling and veering towards, if not depression, something not too dissimilar') and elation when I manage to carve out any time for myself to let the dust of my experiences settle. One day, I write about bumping into somebody I know in town when I'm out with my baby and toddler and bursting into tears. She says that she'll take the children the next day for a couple of hours and I go to a café perched above an old bridge and sit there alone, utterly entranced by and attuned to my surroundings:

To my right I can see the blue sky gathering strength against the November clouds; to my left are people sitting very quietly, drinking cups of tea; behind me I can hear the roar of the cappuccino machine and in front of me there is a smouldering fire, a perfect cup of coffee and a saucer with a biscotti and a small white bowl of sparkling sugar lumps. And why am I focussing on this? The answer is very simple: because I am ALONE, without children.

How much do we lose of ourselves when we have children? Or even when we enter a long-term relationship? Naturally this was my own choice, but I was swept up in motherhood while I was still finding my feet in a fairly new relationship. Two enormous changes happened in a short space of time: I stopped being a single, independent woman and soon after, I was being utterly relied upon by one tiny being, then two, then three. Pregnant, breastfeeding, pregnant, breastfeeding, pregnant, breastfeeding. No breaks from this cycle. Again, I was an adult and I went into this with my eyes open, with free will and choice. But did I know the true emotional and physical toll of this? I was already deeply exhausted by the time I had my second child and yet, somehow (probably because both Andy and I were one of three), we just assumed we would have a third baby. Of course I wouldn't change it now, but my point is that sometimes the current of life overtakes us and we are swept along in such a way that choice is still available to us, yet it doesn't really feel that way. We become powerless to the current; at least, that's how it seems to me in retrospect.

Not long after the day when I sit and drink in my surroundings of the café on the bridge, I write in my diary about four long nights in a row. Andy has to take the day off work to look after the girls because I am in such a bad way that he isn't confident about leaving me with them. I write about being tempted to collapse back into bed, but I know that I am lacking fresh air and Vitamin D and so, encouraged by Andy, I go for a long walk along the Great Ouse Valley Way. After I have walked a long way, I am hit afresh how tired I am and how badly I need to sit down, but there is nowhere but the hard, cold, November ground. However, just as I turn the next corner of the riverbank, the most welcome bench I have ever known appears. I gratefully collapse into it and, after sitting quietly for some time, I take out my diary and pen.

'The plaque on this bench reads 'In Loving Memory of Bill Wavell Grant Garner 7/4/41-20/2/07 – One of his favourite places on the Great River Ouse'. So, thank you Bill... I need to ask for help because somewhere, SOMEWHERE out there is a solution to my insomnia and a bubble filled with sweet dreams and deep slumber that is mine to hold. And so, here I am, sitting on Bill's very welcome and timely bench and I ask everything around me...

Please help me grey and white scudding clouds. Please help me sharp winter sunlight. Please help me busy, twittering birds. Please help me beautiful black lace twigs stencilled against the pale blue sky. Please help me ribbon of river flowing purposefully downstream. Please help me hareem of graceful, bending bullrushes. Please help me gently fading light, mud underfoot, greenorangebrown leaves, pattern coated cows, cawing crows, golden sun winking through the trees, flapping wings, lapping water, bobbing boat, moving sky, spirit of Bill who loved this place...Please help me sleep.

Underneath these words, I have stuck in a small leaf, darkened and curled with the passage of the years. What would I have thought if I had known back then that that thirteen years later, I would still be in the same place? No doubt I would have been horrified, filled with despair. But being able to write when everything else is falling apart, especially when I've found speaking so hard, has been a saving grace for me. It's my gift; my superpower. I see that clearly now. In creating fictional worlds, I've let words rest in my hands, weighing them up like liquid gold to choose the most powerful combination so that when they are held up to the light, they gleam. And then, this memoir. It has been through many incarnations and, in the midst of being dragged down beneath the waves yet again, I finally meet the seabed and from there, I start to write this. For from the very depths, there is only one way to travel.

What began for me as a mere irritation with the odd night of sleeplessness

The Sky Within Rebecca Stonehill

has escalated into a mental health crisis so profound that I am often left gasping for air, unable to still the voices in my head. There was a time when I thought I would write my story from 'the other side.' But this other side, I see now, is a future projection. It may or may not exist but the point is, the time is now. I must write now. I certainly don't pretend to have all the answers and I realise this has been stopping me from committing my story to paper. For how, I have wondered, can I possibly have anything meaningful to say when I remain so mired in uncertainty and challenging emotions? There's so much that I still don't understand. I don't have a magic needle to re-stitch the torn pieces of my life and I cannot untie the strings of a box that contains neat, shiny answers for myself or for anybody reading these words.

But after all these years, here's what I do have: some tools, some practices and the guiding words and inspiration of people who have shone a beacon of light for me through some dark times. Perhaps you have picked up this book because you also are deeply familiar with the effects of chronic insomnia, or it could be that you are reading it on behalf of somebody you care about. I hope that within these pages you can find something here that can shine a light for you too, even if it's the faintest flicker. For every fire begins with the smallest of sparks.

The Story of Thoughts

'We organise our circumstances into stories, stories we pick up along the way and carry with us.
Stories that declare, I'm lacking.
Why me? stories.
I'm alone, stories.
What will I amount to? stories.
Stories about who we should be. Or think we are.
They are interior maps whose familiar roads we travel. Over and over. Yet when we apprehend these maps, these stories, these patterns...we awaken and rise, as it were, to a new perspective, to new possibilities.

Jean-Pierre Weill from *The Well of Being*

I am in London with Andy, waiting for a train to take us back to Norfolk, where we live. I'm feeling tired and low, and as we have a while before our train leaves from Liverpool Street, we decide to go for a pub lunch near the station. I am feeling tired and low; the previous week I received my second driving offence of the year and have to attend a driver offender retraining course. I know I shouldn't drive when I'm so sleep-deprived - back in Nairobi I'd even managed to fall asleep at the wheel, crashing into the back of a bus. I was surprisingly unscathed; the car wasn't though. The more recent experiences have reminded me that this is a lesson I must heed; that I cannot get behind the wheel unless I have a minimum level of my wits about me, not an easy thing to measure. But my inability to drive is one more thing I feel I am losing: my independence and freedom.

As Andy and I walk to the pub, a memory suddenly rises from four years previously when I walked down that exact same street. It was at a time when I had flown back from Nairobi to London not long after the holiday on Wasini Island; my family and I had considered it urgent that I see a number of people over a period of about 10 days who could potentially shine some

The Sky Within Rebecca Stonehill

light on what I was going through. As I recall walking down those same streets, I feel the weight of the past bearing down on my shoulders. My mind immediately snaps into commentary: *four years later and look at me, I'm in exactly the same place. In fact, I'm worse. I'm a wreck. I'm a mess. I don't even want to be out, I just want to go into a quiet room and lie down.* And on and on these attacks on myself relentlessly flow.

But as we sit down at the table in the pub and order food, I ask myself a question: *who would I be without the thought that something is very wrong with me?*

My answer is that I would be a tired woman, out for lunch with her husband. Full stop. And just like that, the heaviness lifts from my shoulders, with the weight of past baggage and future anxiety lifting. It certainly doesn't result in suddenly not being tired, but what it means is that I can breathe more freely and rest in my present existence without the mental pain of what I am going through pulling me into despair.

Incredible, the potency of the stories that my mind tells me. It tells me that I am a bad mother, a terrible wife, an inattentive friend. It tells me that there is so much wrong with me. At various periods, it has done a good job of making me believe that I cannot make plans to meet anyone or do anything out of the house because I may have to cancel due to feeling so awful. My mind is the ultimate spin-doctor and if I buy into the stories I am constantly being told, it causes me a great deal of distress. Meditation and mindfulness courses have exploded all over the globe, for good reason: we do buy into our thoughts. All the time. I know I'm not alone with my mind running riot in this way, a constant stream of narratives and running commentaries on why something is a certain way. We are subjected to a volley of sound bites, memories, conversations and projections of what might happen in the future. Milarepa, a 12th Century Tibetan yogi, wrote countless songs and poems about meditation and the nature of mind. In one song he wrote that *mind has more projections than there are dust motes in a sunbeam...* Our minds, in short, are exhausting!

Clinical Psychologist and meditation teacher Tara Brach frames it this way: she describes our thoughts as being 'Real but not true.' For they do feel so, so, achingly, four-dimensional real. But are they actually true? Quite often, they're not. Whether I believe my thoughts or not; whether I choose to listen to the clamour of my mind, completely changes how I live my life. Greek Stoic philosopher Epictetus (50-135 AD) said, *we are disturbed not by what happens to us, but our thoughts about what happens.* In other words, suffering is amplified as a result of the mind's commentary on the situation, just like that time I was in London with Andy.

This is not an easy statement to contain. What, for example, when we are caught in the ravages of war or chronic illness or have lost a loved one? Surely the reality of this pain is real? Yes, it is real. But our thoughts have the ability to torment us far more than the situation already is. Our thoughts steer our actions, our words, our outlook, our very world view. And yet what if this world view has been warped by being presented with un-truths, and we don't have the tools at our disposal to question the misrepresentation of the truth? Byron Brown, teacher and author says that *you are a slave to your own ideas of who you are and how you need to be.*

So, what do I do when I have a thought that plagues my mind and won't go away? First of all, I recognise that the thought is there and allow myself to feel what I'm feeling. I can't push it away because, like anything else I try to remove, it will wheedle its way deeper into my psyche. Simply by noticing what is arising in my mind and saying to myself 'thinking' is a good place to start.

Not long before that pub lunch in London with Andy, I pull a book from my shelf that a friend game me years ago (but I'd never got around to reading) by a woman named Byron Katie. The book is called *Loving What Is*. In her early forties, as well as being locked in an unhappy marriage, she was struggling with depression, over-eating, agoraphobia as well as alcohol and substance abuse, resulting in a breakdown. But this breakdown led to an epiphany, and Byron Katie developed a method of inquiry that transformed her experience of life and enabled her to make peace with her reality. In turn, her methodology has gone on to help many people around the world. Byron Katie talks about how we question the veracity of our thoughts and, as we do that, we see these perceived 'truths' unravelling before our very eyes. A great proponent of not fighting the reality of our situation, she outlines a system of questioning and remaining alert to our thoughts without battling them. *You can argue with the way things are,* she says. *You'll lose, but only 100% of the time.*

Since reading the book, I have found it helpful to experiment with Byron Katie's four questions, remaining curious to see where the answers may take me. The first question is to ask myself if the particular thought I am having is true. Next, is to ask myself if I can absolutely know that thought is true. Whilst this may sound similar to the first question, it requires a deeper level of inquiry. Now, it could be that I still believe it to be absolutely true – that's fine, it's just a commitment one way or another. With the third question, I ask myself is how I react when I believe that particular thought, paying attention to the specifics of what happens in my body and mind when I buy into the thought. I have to be as honest as possible here: if I am reacting with resentment, anger, deep sadness, whatever it is – it's important I don't try to quieten what is really going on. With the final question, I ask myself who I would be without that thought, and how my life would be different without it. It's helpful at this point to close my eyes and wait; not to grasp at the first thing that comes into my head. Who would I be, really?

It doesn't quite finish there. In fact, Byron Katie's fifth step – though it may feel counter-intuitive – has the power to unlock the greatest wisdom of them all. This is the turning around of the original thought and statement and looking at it in a new light. Imagine my thought is this: I hate having chronic insomnia. There are a few ways this statement can be turned around. For example, I can try this: I don't hate having chronic insomnia.

But wait, I do hate it. I loathe it. I never go out. I hardly see anyone. I cry every day. I've lost my social life. The turnaround is absurd; it doesn't work, does it?

Time to pause and take a deep breath.

What opportunities has this experience given me? It's not what I expected of my life, but that's exactly what causes the distress: when expectations and reality don't align. This is painful, raw work. But if you are reading these words and you are aware that your thoughts cause you to suffer, I urge you to try it out. Grab a pen or pencil because the power of the written word and committing to paper is important here. Let me share my own list I once made when I asked myself this question. This was written during a period when self-esteem and energy levels were so low I struggled to leave the house for days on end. Here it is, unedited, in the order I wrote it:

I love my insomnia because
    I get to rest a lot during the day
    I can watch the beauty of the changing seasons through the window
    It has encouraged me to write poetry
    It has helped me to be more compassionate
    Everything feels so much more alive for me on my good days than if I felt great every day

It has made me dig deep into my inner life
It has introduced me to some profound, life-changing books
It means I get to listen to René (my great friend) reading a book to me in installments on *WhatsApp*
It has made me be very honest with myself
It has strengthened my connection with nature
It has helped me to be a good listener and friend on the good days
It has made me realise how strong I am, because I can still write
Over to you.

What thought is endemic to you right now?

Is this thought true?

Can you absolutely know it's true?

How do you react when you believe that thought?

Who would you be without that thought?

Now, turn it around. Write down your unedited thoughts.

The frame through which I have viewed my experiences all these years has most definitely changed its form depending on the tone of my personal narrative. I can be feeling reasonable, yet I suffer because of the larger story my mind tells me; conversely, I can be extremely tired but a calmness is still able to settle around me and a small voice says: this is your experience. What is it you need right now? Recognising our thoughts for what they are is a lifelong work. The more we practise, catching those thought patterns in a net before they weave themselves into the fabric of our identities and our stories, the more we can gently separate from what is true and what blends into myth.

The Sky Within Rebecca Stonehill

Coeur

'How do you do it?' said night.
How do you wake up and shine?
I keep it simple, said light.
One day at a time.'

Lemn Sissay, Author & Poet

The anxiety comes at the quietest of times, when the incessant hum of traffic and murmur of voices or birdsong has ceased: Night. It always comes at night.

And after one particular night, that feels as though it stretches from the creation of the universe almost fourteen billion years ago until the present moment, Andy sees the children off to school, gets me in the car and drives me to the Accident & Emergency unit of the local hospital. As the doctor reads through my notes, I can feel a frown on her face without even looking at her. 'Could you try and explain in your own words why you are here?'

There is a pause and I feel the warm grasp of Andy's hand over mine. I glance at him; I don't need to say anything. He knows I have the words inside me but I can't get them out.

'I'm going to talk because… because she finds it difficult to. I had to bring her because of the kinds of things she was saying last night.

'What was she saying?'

'She was saying…' I feel an involuntary squeeze of my hand. 'She was saying that she didn't want to be alive anymore. That she couldn't be alive anymore. She said that she could hear voices, telling her to finish it all.'

'I see.'

The Sky Within Rebecca Stonehill

I stare at a crack on the wall above her head. I don't want to be here.

'Rebecca. Please can you look at me? No, I mean, straight at me. I need you to make eye contact, please. I need to hear this from you. These voices – was it your voice or somebody else's?'

I stare at her, stricken. I don't know. I can't remember. I shake my head.

'Rebecca. Were you seriously considering taking your own life last night?'

It hurts to hear it being said as plainly as that and tears pool in my eyes. I nod.

'Pills? Jumping out of the window? In front of traffic?'

I wince. All I can focus on is the heavy warmth of Andy's hand over mine.

'I know this is difficult, Rebecca. But please answer me if you can. I'm here to help you.'

I try to talk and it comes out as a rasp. I clear my throat, the tears now flowing freely. 'I don't know,' I say, my voice barely above a whisper. 'Last night it probably would have been the window. I need more pills. I need something more to help me sleep.'

Again, the frown as she flicks back over the notes. 'The trouble is that you're already taking incredibly strong sleeping pills and I can see that...' she peers over the top of her glasses, 'that this is in combination with your anti-depressant.'

'But the sleeping pills don't work. The anti-depressants don't work. Nothing is working.' My voice comes out in a strangled sob and Andy makes circular motions around my back.

'It's alright, Rebecca,' she says in a kind voice and half-smiles at me, handing me a box of tissues. 'I think we need to get you off these anti-depressants and perhaps try...' she pauses, bites her bottom lip. 'But actually no, you've already tried that one. Ok, and that one. And...'.

The doctor's voice trails off and I can feel her staring at me.

'Is your wife having counselling?' she asks Andy. He nods.

'Well, clearly these anti-depressants are not doing anything for her. So I'd like her to slowly come off them. As for the sleeping pills – '

'Please give me something stronger. Please.'

We stare at one another, the doctor and I, and I feel as though I am transmitting the desperation of my request from my being into hers. There is a silent standoff as she narrows her eyes, exhaling slowly.

'Alright,' she says eventually. 'Leave it with me.'

And herein, you see, lies a compounding problem. Faced with a woman who has been brought into A&E by her husband because she can't breathe, because she is hearing voices, because she is threatening suicide, what is a doctor to do? The woman desperately needs sleep, the kind of deep sleep of oblivion, that much is clear. At least that would ensure that she wakes up clearer headed and more able to think through the next steps. She is already having therapy and she has tried for many months, sometimes even years various combinations of anti-depressant medication, with no lasting impact. Again, I ask, what is a doctor to do? She did what most doctors would have done, and she agreed to more sleeping pills in a stronger combination. These pills, I was told, would knock me out; that it was not possible they wouldn't.

And so there I had it, a few nights of that sleep of oblivion that my body and soul craved so deeply. But of course I knew, Andy knew, the doctor knew, that it was a sticking plaster. It wasn't even real sleep, it was a simulated, enforced sleep and what had not been put in place was this simple two-worded question: what next?

What next indeed? That night on the clifftop in Wasini, I didn't really want to die. Just as I didn't want to the night before I sat in A&E with Andy, nor the other similar times I have been through since. I just wanted a different life, a life I could call meaningful. I was deeply grieving a loss of joy, a loss of spontaneity and connection. But, for now, this was the life I had, and how to keep going when I was dragged down again and again? According to Francis Weller, *any loss, whether deeply personal or one of those that swirl around us in the wider world, calls us to full-heartedness, for that is the meaning of courage.*

The Sky Within Rebecca Stonehill

Yes. Courage. I needed it in spades, when I felt like this trait couldn't have been further from my core and my heart felt like an empty shell. Life seemed to encompass being in constant survival model; that even to get through the day was an enormous achievement, never mind about anything else. Everything felt like a gargantuan, insurmountable task, even simple things like getting out of bed and getting dressed. I knew that somehow I had to get through the next hour and then the next, and the next again. But even that, I just didn't know how I was going to do it.

I simply didn't know how I would navigate this mire of grief. A quick sidenote here on this word, 'grief.' It is often linked with an intense and overpowering emotion we feel upon losing someone close to us. Perhaps it is most commonly felt with this loss, but it has many channels and origins. The Oxford Dictionary describes grief as 'deep or intense sorrow' and if we rewind time and peel back the word's etymological laters, we find an old thirteenth century French word *grever* meaning afflict, burden, oppress. Origins also lie in the Latin word *gravare* which means to make heavy.

To make heavy. Heaviness. Yes, I know this feeling so well.

The days I mentioned earlier I call the 'letterbox' days, for a very simple reason. There is a red letterbox that sits on the pavement on the opposite side of the road from my house, a little further down. It takes approximately thirty seconds to walk to that letterbox. But there have been many days when walking there to post a letter (or even just walking to it in order to get out of the house) have felt synonymous to scaling Everest. Sometimes I have had to sit for a long time by the front door to even summon the courage to leave my house. On these days, I feel so swamped by sadness, it's difficult to believe that life can be another way; that if I can't even walk thirty seconds down the road to a letterbox, how will I ever be able to carry out more meaningful activities?

So, what exactly is available when I am in the midst of emotions so overpowering they threaten to overwhelm me? If I feel a panic attack coming, I can't stop crying or my sadness feels too much to bear? First of all, my breath is always there, and when I stop whatever I'm doing and breathe, I can re-anchor myself to my body. When we are feeling very low, we tend to contract and not breathe properly. But this is a time when we need to draw upon the precious ability of our lungs and abdomen to breathe deeply and fully. At no other time could our breath be more important.

Rabbi Alan Lew says that *our breath connects us to the level of experience that is deeper than speech, deeper than the forms speech creates – not the word for the thing, but the thing itself.*

I find it helpful to then imagine somebody I love and care for deeply is in distress. How would I treat them at this time? What would I say to them? The way we respond to a friend in deep suffering is exactly the same as the way we need to treat ourselves: with kindness, tenderness and compassion. *Rather than indulge or reject our experience*, says Buddhist teacher Pema Chödrön, *we can somehow let the energy of the emotion, the quality of what we're feeling, pierce us to the heart.*

Despair feels profound, and all-consuming. It can threaten to pull us deep to the bottom of the ocean with no conceivable way to surface again. Poet David Whyte describes despair as ...*a season, a waveform passing through the body, not a prison surrounding us.* Imagine this, if it were not the prison it feels like, but an energy that is passing through our bodies? Whyte also looks at a gentle antidote to despair, suggesting that *it is not to be found in the brave attempt to cheer ourselves up with happy abstracts, but in paying a profound and courageous attention to the body and the breath, independent of our imprisoning thoughts and stories...*

I find great comfort in his words. I'm not going to just 'get over this.' No. I am going to take the courageous step of seeing what is happening inside me. I am going to keep breathing and checking in with how my body feels in this moment. Brené Brown is a researcher who has written a number of best-selling books on courage and vulnerability. She says that *courage starts with showing up and letting ourselves be seen.* I have realised over the years just how painful it is to stand in the full light of an open window and allow myself to be seen for what is truly happening to me. I have become a master of subterfuge; of excuses for cancelled plans and a canny ability to swerve around questions.

There is a question that people ask that goes something along the lines of How are you? Are you well? On the surface, it sounds like a heartfelt inquiry but, in reality, it leaves little room for more than one answer. How many times I have longed to breathe truth into a response, but have not found the courage to do so. It's not the 'done thing' to share too much and here in the UK in particular, we are very, very good at masking our emotions and getting on with things. I don't know who coined the phrase Keep Buggering On, or KBO as it is more euphemistically known, but this phrase was a favourite amongst my grandparents' generation and has certainly been

The Sky Within Rebecca Stonehill

passed down the family line to their own children of the baby-boomer generation in which anything other than that would be self-indulgent. The world we live in is results-driven, in which we strive to be better, to do more, to constantly achieve, to keep busy at all costs. Often we associate the word 'courage' with this personal quest to go beyond our boundaries and run bravely in the face of fire. And yes, sometimes we must step beyond our safety zones we have pencilled in around ourselves. The etymology of the word courage from the old Norman French, is *coeur*, heart. If we are looking inwards and acting with full-heartedness, or simply with 'heart', sometimes the most courageous act we take can be the one that feels most counter-intuitive: to acknowledge our suffering, allowing it to be seen by ourselves and by others.

According to psychologist Carl Rogers, *it wasn't until I accepted myself just as I was, that I was free to change.* This doesn't mean not taking action; it means moving forwards from a place of recognition, almost like pulling down a veil between ourselves and that painful thing we'd rather not look at. We are called to witness what we are going through on a deep, visceral level and from that still, soft space, we consider our response. *May I meet this moment fully,* says author and psychotherapist Sylvia Boorstein. *May I meet it as a friend.* Another way to think about it is a gentle practice of accepting our experience. There are many people who, in a show of alpha strength, set out to remove all obstacles to happiness in order to 'fix' things. In an age of positive thinking and the law of attraction whereby our positivity can be manifested, acceptance can often be seen as a passive stance; that the person in turmoil is not taking the necessary decisive steps to relieve their troubles. Our social media feeds are a stark reflection of this; we are allowed to be sad, but woe betide the person who stays sad for too long and perhaps it would be better if that person retreated for a while until they have something more cheerful to impart. As Katherine May says in her book on the power of rest and retreat in difficult times, *Wintering*: *this is where we are now: endlessly cheerleading ourselves into positivity, while erasing the dirty underside of real life.*

In a twist of the human heart, could an acceptance of our experiences ultimately lead to the suffering releasing its grip? This is not to say that we don't believe positive change is possible. Author Byron Brown says *acceptance does not mean you approve of your experience, think it's OK, like it, or are happy with it as it is… acceptance is not an expression of any kind of evaluation or interpretation. It simply means you can allow your experience to be exactly as it is.* If we believe this, perhaps acceptance is the most courageous and radical step we can take in the face of suffering, bringing a tender presence to our hardships. Acknowledging that we are struggling unites us as a member of the human family with all the limitations this brings. Rumi, 13th Century Persian poet, certainly understood this when he urged his fellow citizens to stay with what wounds us:

> *Don't turn away.*
> *Keep your gaze on*
> *the bandaged place.*
> *That's where the*
> *light enters you.*

Fast forward seven hundred years, and visionary musician Leonard Cohen expresses the very same sentiment in his song, *Anthem*:

> *Ring the bells that still can ring*
> *Forget your perfect offering*
> *There is a crack, a crack in everything*
> *That's how the light gets in.*

As the doctor writes me out a prescription for stronger sleeping pills and we bid one another farewell, something wordless passes between us: it is a tacit acknowledgment that we both know these pills are very far from being a solution. Andy and I drive home in the car, the world streaming past me in all its noise and colour. I watch life happening on the other side and a calm descends upon me, the type of calm that often comes after an emotional storm. I can get through this, I think to myself, but what if I have to be with whatever is happening? As I wipe a tear away, I feel a deep-boned weariness of the longevity of this. I know that I so badly don't want to be with it, but here are my options right at this moment: fight what 'is' and feel worse. Or feel what I am going through, recognise where I am at and see what I am capable of.

Rachel Naomi Remen is a writer, integrative medicine practitioner and founder of the Remen Institute for the Study of Health and Illness. She makes a distinction between 'healing' and being 'cured' of what it is that afflicts a person physically and mentally. She talks about how being cured refers to repair, particularly on the physical level. Healing, on the other hand, speaks of growth and this can be mental, emotional, physical, and a combination of all of these and more. It is finding a place of human wholeness which expands our ability to engage with life, in spite of our

The Sky Within Rebecca Stonehill

physical wounds. In Rachel Naomi Remen's own words: *healing happens at the level of the person and involves an evolution and refinement of the individual, a deepening of the capacity for emotional life, mental life and spiritual life and the furthering of personal wholeness and not physical health.*

As I was finding in my own situation, this can be hard to recognise when we want so badly to be cured. But it takes courage and wisdom to recognise the distinction between curing and healing. But what does it actually mean to heal? The truth is, it doesn't always mean what we expect it to. It doesn't necessarily mean that we are free from a chronic condition, or that we don't feel the crushing blow of losing somebody. Though our shiny magazines and social media feeds would like to tell otherwise, the fact that I have been intimate with such anguish, that I am grieving or 'falling apart' or broken-hearted; the truth is that there is nothing 'wrong' with me. My tears signal that I am alive and that my heart beats strongly inside me. And part of healing is to express this sadness. As Francis Weller says: *grief is essential to finding and maintaining a feeling of emotional intimacy with life.*

We wouldn't be human if we didn't want to feel better and for the burden that weighs so heavily on our shoulders to be eased. But when grief and sadness come knocking at our doors, it is a test, but also a kind of healing. In the words of Pema Chödrön, *we think that the point is to pass the test or to overcome the problem, but the truth is that things don't really get solved. They come together and fall apart again. It's just like that. The healing comes from letting there be room for all this to happen: room for grief, for relief, for misery, for joy.*

I'd like to include here the passage of joy and sorrow from American Lebanese Writer Kahlil Gibran's seminal work, *The Prophet*. It can take a few readings of *On Joy and Sorrow* for the truth of these words to sink and settle, but once they do, we can see how joy and sorrow, in reality, are inseparable and how one is not 'better' than the other. When I truly understood the sentiment and the hidden power behind Gibran's words, I wept with relief and gratitude.

Your joy is your sorrow unmasked.
And the selfsame well from which your laughter rises was oftentimes filled with your tears.
And how else can it be?
The deeper that sorrow carves into your being, the more joy you can contain.
Is not the cup that holds your wine the very cup that was burned in the potter's oven?
And is not the lute that soothes your spirit, the very wood that was hollowed with knives?
When you are joyous, look deep into your heart and you shall find it is only that which has

given you sorrow that is giving you joy.
When you are sorrowful look again in your heart, and you shall see that in truth you are weeping for that which has been your delight.

Some of you say, "Joy is greater than sorrow," and others say, "Nay, sorrow is the greater."

But I say unto you, they are inseparable.
Together they come, and when one sits, alone with you at your board, remember that the other is asleep upon your bed.

Verily you are suspended like scales between your sorrow and your joy.
Only when you are empty are you at standstill and balanced.
When the treasure-keeper lifts you to weigh his gold and his silver, needs must your joy or your sorrow rise or fall.

On Joy and Sorrow by Kahlil Gibran

In my early twenties, I spent two years living and working in Granada in Southern Spain. This was a period during which I felt intensely alive. I lived in an apartment with a colourful assortment of people from different countries and I felt fully immersed in the experience of learning Spanish; taking long walks through what, for me, remains one of the most beautiful cities on earth; staying up late with my housemates and exchanging ideas; going for tapas; hosting parties; going to parties; finding new places to go dancing.

Of course I was aware at the time that I was having fun, and I took full advantage of every new experience that came my way. But every time I returned to Spain since those two vibrant years that I spent there, I would feel a dull, unnameable ache in my chest. More recently, with the difficulties with my health more pervasive, the ache took on a more dramatic tone on the infrequent occasions I would visit Spain. Being there, I realised that I was suffering greatly, even more so than I had been back at home. Why was this? It was because I was weeping for that which had been my delight.

This was not simply nostalgia or regret for my lost youth; nor was it only as a result of the bone-aching weariness that kept me company. The tears that fell did so because Spain had, for many years, been a symbol of joy, of levity, of joie de vivre. I felt that pain because my experiences in that country had

The Sky Within Rebecca Stonehill

nurtured me and given me so much joy. As a young woman in her early twenties, I had taken all the pleasures that Granada had to offer me, mostly unthinkingly. I cannot say that I appreciated every single moment of those nurturing months there, because I took freely of the experiences I believed to be rightfully mine. At that stage in my life, I hadn't known deep suffering and so it was impossible for it to be otherwise.

But now, with adversity placed irrevocably in my back pocket, I am able to embrace the experiences that are now gifted to me in a way I couldn't as a young woman. I can never return to those days of carefree mirth. But perhaps, one day, I can travel to Granada armed with this new layer of wisdom and a clear image of joy and suffering on either side of the scales, balanced in perfect, inseparable harmony.

The pain that will be felt from being with our sorrows can threaten to overwhelm us, yet when we allow ourselves to really feel these emotions, the possibility for something to gently shift opens up. Tara Brach likes to tell a story whereby the great Tibetan Yogi Milarepa is living in isolation in a mountain cave where he meditates, often seeing the contents of his mind as visible projections. On one occasion, his cave is filled with a great number of demons. One in particular is being persistent and aggressive, so Milarepa decides to do something different: he puts his head into the mouth of the demon. And at that very moment, a moment of surrender, all of the demons fade and vanish. This is a powerful image: not just skirting around the outside of what assails us, but actually going right inside it. It is an act of tremendous courage and may initially bring more pain than we imagined possible, but if we go to this place, given time and patience, the demons may begin to fade. Francis Weller describes the way we crawl into the heart of our experience thus: *we must turn towards our experience and touch it with the softest hands possible. Only then, in the inner terrain of silence and solitude, will our grief yield to us and offer up its most tender shoots.*

It takes tremendous courage to say YES to the painful parts of our lives. There have been so many times when I have thought absolutely not, I don't want to sit with these painful emotions. I've had enough of this. I don't want to do this inner work anymore. I don't want to be a burden any longer. Enough. These conflicting emotions when I am trying to say yes, but I'm not winning, can feel completely overwhelming. It has resulted many times in a flood of anger and deep, all-consuming grief.

At the same time, I do believe in my own innate courage. I believe that we all have that kernel of strength rooted deep inside of us that never goes away. Each and every one of us. Growing up, I was always fascinated by Mexican painter Frida Kahlo: by her bright, metaphorical paintings, her bohemian clothes and piercing eyes gazing out from beneath thick brows. Kahlo endured lifelong pain and injuries from a bus accident, but this precise pain fuelled her most celebrated creative work. *At the end of the day,* she said, *we can endure much more than we think.*

I have questioned that in my most difficult moments. Can I really endure more? I have had to hold that 'NO', breathe into it and wait until it becomes a YES. This is the bravest act imaginable. It is the most courageous act of them all. Brené Brown has written powerfully on the role that courage can play in our lives. She speaks of the courage it takes to allow ourselves to feel pain and the necessity of not sweeping our vulnerabilities beneath the carpet but, rather, allowing these very vulnerabilities to act as our agents of change. *Wholehearted living,* she writes, *is about engaging in our lives from a place of worthiness. It means cultivating the courage, compassion and connection to wake up in the morning and think, no matter what gets done and how much is left undone, I am enough. It's going to bed at night thinking, Yes, I am imperfect and vulnerable and sometimes afraid, but that doesn't change the truth that I am also brave and worthy of love and belonging.*

In my own experience, I have often felt as though I have no choice available to me, because I have no control over these feelings that are so powerful and all-consuming. This, however, is a myth. There is always a choice, if we can only find the courage within to recognise it. Jewish psychologist and survivor of three Nazi concentration camps, Viktor Frankl, said that *everything can be taken from a man but one thing: the last of the human freedoms — to choose one's attitude in any given set of circumstances, to choose one's own way.* Frankl watched as hundreds of people that he knew perished. Yet despite the horrors unfolding around him he resolved to believe, he *chose* to believe that there was more than a single outcome to his experience.

Sitting in the A&E department of the hospital with Andy that day, it is hard to believe in that moment that there is more than one outcome to what I am going through. I am so deeply mired in despair that I cannot see beyond my experience; that this is my lot in life and things will never be another way.

Deep breath. Take courage, heart. I extend compassion to that self from my past who is gripped by fear and anxiety in the quiet of the night; who sits sobbing in a hospital room and who has been pulled beneath the waves

The Sky Within Rebecca Stonehill

again and again. For even in the midst of this, there exists within me a knowing and a truth of who I am and what step I must take. It can be so hard to trust this, particularly when layers of grief and suffering cloak my wisest self. But I am still learning with the gift of *coeur* and slow, steady, gentle practice that I carry the strength I need within me, pulsing steady as a heartbeat.

There is no controlling life.
Try corralling a lightning bolt,
containing a tornado. Dam a
stream and it will create a new
channel. Resist, and the tide
will sweep you off your feet.

Allow, and grace will carry
you to higher ground. The only
safety lies in letting it all in — the wild and the weak;
fear, fantasies, failures and success.
When loss rips off the doors of
your heart, or sadness veils your
vision with despair, practice
becomes simply bearing the truth.

In the choice to let go of your
known way of being, the whole
world is revealed to your new eyes.

Allow by Danna Faulds

The Sky Within Rebecca Stonehill

Gold Dust

'The richest relationships are lifeboats, but they are also submarines that descend to the darkest and most disquieting places, to the unfathomed trenches of the soul where our deepest shames and foibles and vulnerabilities live, where we are less than we would like to be.'

Maria Popova, Writer & Blogger

My middle child is beside herself with excitement because her godmother, one of my oldest and dearest of friends, is taking her to see the Harry Potter play of *The Cursed Child* in London. Andy is abroad travelling with work and my other children are staying with friends. I'm going through a really bad patch but I know that there's no question about it – I have to make it to London the next day with my daughter.

At this point I am on anti-depressants which are not doing much for me, but I can't just suddenly come off them. To be on the safe side, I decide to take double sleeping pills, assuming I will sleep and be alright the following day. But I don't, and I'm not. Taking double is a mistake; not only am I sleep deprived, but I also feel the pulse of a deep headache and an indiscernible thrum of something else settling in beneath my temples: brain fog, confusion and fear. I don't know if I can make it to London.

But how can I let my daughter down? I force myself to stand under a cold shower and throw some snacks together for the train and we walk to the station. She is chattering animatedly: this is my child of kaleidoscopic enthusiasms; turn her just a fraction of another way and she will have an entirely different myriad of projects, of things to talk about, of places she wants to go and things she wants to do. Life is never dull, nor quiet, with my middle child. As we sit on the train, the world whirring past us outside the window, I remember her asking me to French plait her hair. I've never much been one of those mothers who neatly brushes and arranges their children's

The Sky Within Rebecca Stonehill

hair, but I comply. At least, I try to as I attempt to look beyond the fog that envelops me. I even remember the finished result: an unruly zigzag of blond braid. My daughter, unperturbed, demands that I take photos. She chatters exuberantly on and as the train hurtles away from Norfolk, I lean my head back against the seat and close my eyes.

I am overwhelmed by everything in London compared to comparatively much quieter, smaller Norwich: the noise, the buildings, the beggars that seem to sit everywhere holding signs imploring passers-by to help. Somehow, we make it to the Palace Theatre in the West End and I hand my daughter over to my old friend. She looks into my eyes and she can see that I'm not alright, but what can she do? She and my daughter have a play to go to. The second the ornate doors of the building swallow the two of them, I burst into tears. I don't know how long I stand outside as theatre-goers walk past me, tears streaming down my face. But eventually, I know that I need to move. The play is around five hours in total, with a break in the middle when we will meet for lunch. Ordinarily, I'd relish that time: I'd go to a museum or an art gallery or perhaps arrange to meet a friend. I know that today I can't do anything of those things, but I do need to find something to do, though I have no idea what shape this will take.

So I start walking. My feet move me around Soho, past bars and restaurants and theatres. I walk past a bookshop and manage to pass an hour in there. But after that? I don't know what to do but walk again. I can't seem to stop crying; every time I think it has dried up it comes again, a fresh burst of grief and exhaustion that courses through my body and I find myself leaning against railings and the sides of buildings, my sunglasses firmly wrapped around my face so I don't have to make eye contact with anybody.

Eventually, the time arrives when my friend and daughter are having the break and we've arranged to meet for a late lunch in a restaurant. As we sit in the brightly-lit, tastefully decorated dining area, my daughter regales me with tales of the amazing set and the lighting and the brilliant actors and how wonderful everything is. I am so happy to hear all this and to see them; finally, I can stop my endless pacing around the streets of central London. The waitress comes over to take our order but suddenly, just like that, I feel it building up from my throat and I know I am going to start crying. Do not, I tell myself. Do not cry. This is my daughter's day, this is not fair on her. Enough. Just get through this day. Enough.

And try as I might to talk myself out of it, to be strong for my daughter's sake, the tears cannot be stemmed. I squeeze my eyes shut and they keep coming, more and more, splashing over the tabletop like the monsoon rains. I hear the waitress clear her throat and say she will come back and I feel my friend's hand over mine, squeezing and rubbing. I don't know how long I sit there for with my eyes closed but eventually, I know I have to open them. I know I have to look at my daughter. It's hard to read the face of this child of mine whose every emotion is usually sketched in indelible ink into each beautiful feature. Can I read horror there? Compassion? Shame? Emapthy? Irritation? A tear forms in the corner of her eye and I ease my hand out from beneath my friends and scoop up my child's hand in both my own, entwining my fingers into hers and bringing them to my lips to kiss them.

'I'm sorry,' I whisper. 'I'm sorry.'

She takes a deep inhale as we stare at each other and I notice her throat contracting as she pushes down emotion.

The rest of the day is a blur. My friend and daughter return to the theatre to watch the second half of the play and I begin my interminable pacing once again. I feel as though I walk up and down every street of Soho during those strange, painful, twilight hours. There are times when I know I can't take another step and I stop behind buildings, in dimly-lit alleyways as brick walls keep me upright, my eyes closed. I think I even drop off a few times, my head lolling uncomfortably. These pauses help to give me a little more energy and I begin walking again, passing the glass windows of people in restaurants and bars, bringing cutlery to their mouths or throwing their heads back in laughter. Everything is in slow motion, a thick soup of dislocation. I feel as though I am stuck in a purgatory of no return – that I have always been pacing the streets of London and will never be able to stop.

But the day, like every day, eventually closes. My daughter, despite the episode in the restaurant, says it's been one of her best days ever and we make it back to Norfolk. The memories of that Saturday will always arise edged with pain, but another memory seems to push ahead of the most difficult aspect of it: the warmth of my friend's hand over mine and the understanding I read in her eyes. She was there for me. Without question.

As Maria Popova articulates in the quote at the start of this chapter, we may be *less than we would like to be* during dark times, but we will all go through episodes in our lives where we find ourselves staring out at the sky from the

The Sky Within Rebecca Stonehill

depths of the trenches, unsure of how to make the journey back towards the light. I've realised over the years that a vocabulary of pleasantries exists universally in our vernacular; for the births, the marriages and the promotions and so on – to congratulate and celebrate. And it is right that these jubilant events should be responded to in kind. And yet, what I have come to notice more and more is that, by contrast, there is a great poverty of emotional intelligence vocabulary to mark periods or moments of suffering. This, despite the fact that it is a universal condition, in much the same vein as joy that every person on our planet experiences. Whereas the joyous moments are met with a language of celebration, the dark spaces of grief are very often met with a deafening silence or unsolicited advice that can wound the sufferer more than comfort them. We do not possess the necessary words to know how to respond, so we don't respond at all, or we respond with unintentional insensitivity.

When we are having a hard time, we often want to be alone. I have certainly spent a great deal of time in that space, not wanting to be a burden and also not feeling the strength or ability to reach out to others. And yet, we must. *Community is society with a human face*, writes Rabbi Jonathan Sacks, *the place where we know we're not alone.* I have had to break down barriers over the years, to sandpaper away the edges of my pride to ask for help and also, simply, to build those pillars of necessary support around me. *We need support*, says Brené Brown. *We need folks who will let us try on new ways of being without judging us.*

Our ancestors instinctively knew that sorrow and grieving was something to share with the community, with rituals and ceremonies in place to hold people in their suffering. In many parts of the world, grief is still a communal affair. Living in India many years ago, our house-help tragically lost her young son to a preventable illness. Going to her home, I was struck by the number of people filling her small house. They were not just family members but her neighbours; her community, spending time with her, grieving with her, cooking for her and holding her when she needed to be held. *We don't really get close to others*, says Archbishop Desmond Tutu, *if our relationship is made up of unending hunky-dory-ness. It is the hard times, the painful times, the sadness and the grief that knit us more closely together.*

Even when we are not talking about the death of a loved one, we see illness and suffering as a personal problem and we wear this ability to 'get over' what we are going through alone as a badge of honour. I'll be alright. I'll get there. I hear myself say it all the time. And yet, our souls yearn for that communion; that need to be held during dark times. But all too often we ignore that need, perhaps for the reasons I mentioned above: not wanting to burden others or not knowing how to share our grief.

A close friend once used an analogy with me of The Three Kings with their unique offerings of gold, frankincense and myrrh being similar to the gifts that can be brought to relationships. You probably have some friends or family members who bring you Frankincense or Myrrh; these are people who you can have fun with; have a history with; go out with or enjoy chatting to. They feed you in a certain way and you need and appreciate them in your lives.

And then there are the people in our lives who bring us gold. In the ancient Celtic world, they were known as Anam Cara, or friends of the soul, and in the Buddhist tradition they are the *Kalyana-mitra*, the 'noble friend', who will not accept you for anything less than what you truly are. These friends are there for us in dark times as well as light. They see us for who and what we are and with them, we can be comfortable, honest, open, vulnerable and raw. Shakespeare said, *the friends thou hast, and their adoption tried, grapple them to thy soul with hoops of steel.* I don't think Shakespeare was referring to any old friends. His words are attributed to those friends who bring us gold; who are gold-dust.

Having a hard time for several months, for a year even, friends will be there for us. As the months turn into years, they start to fall away. If we ratchet up well over a decade, we are very lucky if we can count friends whose presence we truly feel on the fingers of one hand. Although it can feel painful at times – it certainly has been for me, a person who used to view themselves as very sociable, this circle of support is enough. I like to think of the beautiful image of Stonehenge, ancient stones standing firm in a circle around me. These people who offer me the gift of gold know what it is that we are going through and are there for us, just like my daughter's godmother, my old friend. Another one of these friend's lights candles for me and has read countless books over *WhatsApp* in installments. Hearing her voice is instantly calming. These friends bear witness to our suffering without trying to 'fix' us. They will let us simply cry and will be present for us. *We can count on so few people*, writes poet Adrienne Rich, *to go that hard way with us.* Whoever these people are, if they live close by, they are there to give us a hug or sit with us in our grief. Or if they are on the other side of the country or globe, this is a virtual-togetherness: words, love, time spent hearing one another's voices. Anne Lamott, in the face of alcohol addiction, wrote that *what saved me was*

The Sky Within Rebecca Stonehill

that I found gentle, loyal and hilarious companions, which is at the heart of meaning: maybe we don't find a lot of answers to life's tougher questions, but if we find a few true friends, that's even better. In a similar vein, Rachel Naomi Remen says that we *simply listen generously to someone, not in order to position ourselves or even to understand what is being said. We listen just to know what is true for this person at this moment in time; to witness it and validate it and accept it.*

It's important when we are suffering to identify who our 'gold' friends are. Be very careful about this inner circle during tough times: it's not always the most obvious people. According to Linda Green, psychotherapist and neuroscientist, *The process of being seen, understood, and accepted by an attuned, empathic other engenders a sense of genuine self-acceptance, a feeling that we are profoundly okay. We feel safe enough, strong enough, sure enough to venture courageously into the world and develop the competencies we need to deal with life's challenges.*

Something else to bear in mind when I've been going through a very difficult time, is to keep things close. What I mean by this is that it's wise to not venture verbally outside of my circle of support until I'm ready. In talking about it before this point, something can be lost and I end up feeling more vulnerable. I am under absolutely no obligation to tell people how I'm feeling if I don't feel that safe space with them. Recognising who these few people are in my life has been key; acknowledging them with a life-affirming gratitude and keeping them as close pillars of support. That day in London may have been very difficult physically and emotionally, but knowing I had a person who really saw me has altered the memory of those experiences, so that tenderness and care sit beside the pain.

The Sky Within

'You can search throughout the entire universe for someone who is more deserving of your love and affection than you are yourself, and that person is not to be found anywhere. You, yourself, as much as anybody in the entire universe, deserve your love and affection.'

Buddha

It is the summer of 2019 and I am driving around Northern France with my family in our thirty-year old motorhome. The windows keep falling inwards, the wood-fittings are peeling and the petrol gauge has broken so we have to make sure we know how many miles we have driven in order to ensure we fill up the tank in time. But alongside this, we are stopping in villages for croissants of which even the smallest seems to have a *boulangerie*; we are parking up for the night in forests, on beaches and on clifftops and swimming in the sea in the morning; we are listening to the tinny sound of cassette tapes Andy and I have salvaged from our own childhoods and teenage years. Not unlike my experience on Wasini Island a few years previously, I know that these days should be joyful, vibrant living, for the places we are visiting are alive, vital, picturesque, memorable. And yet, there is a gaping void inside me that no amount of rustic French scenery or delicious food can fill. I am exhausted, physically and emotionally. At one stage, I beg Andy to leave me somewhere in a hotel so my family can continue the trip without what I perceive as my burdensome weight accompanying them from one place to the next.

Andy refuses and onwards we trundle in our motorhome: more *baguettes*; more *café crème*'s in squares; more card games of Phase Ten at night as mosquitos buzz around our ankles. Uncharacteristically, I read only one book this holiday several times over, hugging it to my chest when I'm not devouring its words and scribbling down notes as it's a library book and I can't make any markings inside. It is called *An Interrupted Life: The Diaries and Letters of Etty Hillesum 1941-43* and I vividly remember the look and feel

The Sky Within Rebecca Stonehill

of it. Published by Persephone Books, it has an unprepossessing, pale grey cover with a white band containing the title. I pick it up in the library before we leave and have plenty of other books with me. But I can't tear myself away from this one. For within its unflamboyant pages, I crawl beneath the skin of one mesmerising young woman, long gone, whose greatest wish was to be a writer and who was murdered by the Nazi regime in 1943. You'd be forgiven for thinking this may not be the most cheerful reading material for a woman struggling to contain the riptide of emotions that severe sleep deprivation brings. But her letters and diary entries could not possibly comprise less of a misery memoir. Within these pages, all I find is joy, love and the appreciation of beauty. As our journey progresses through Normandy and deep into the Brittany countryside, I come to know this young woman profoundly and feel nothing but gratitude for the manner in which her words are able to stretch across time and space to infiltrate that tender space of my hurting soul. As I read Etty's lines, and in between her lines, again and again, I keep thinking of the words of poet Mary Oliver: *I read the way a person might swim, to save his or her life.* I understand these words during my time in France in a way I never really have done before for, in many ways, Etty saves me that summer.

Whilst Anne Frank watched the persecution of Jews unfolding in Amsterdam, recording her reactions in her much-famed diary, across the city a twenty-seven year old Jewish woman was writing her own impressions of life, love and persecution. Etty Hillesum knew precisely what was happening across Europe to her fellow Jews. She knew they were being rounded up and that one soul after another was being snuffed out in brutal concentration camps. The remarkable thing about reading Etty's letters and diaries is that she does find beauty in the world within and without, despite the horrors unfolding around her each and every day. The following passage beautifully illustrates her generosity of spirit:

This morning I cycled along the Station Quay enjoying the broad sweep of the sky at the edge of the city and breathing in the fresh, unrationed air. And everywhere signs barring Jews from the paths and the open country. But above the one narrow path still left to us stretches the sky, intact. They can't do anything to us, they really can't... We may be sad and depressed about what is being done to us; that is only human and understandable. However, the greatest injury is one we inflict on ourselves. I find life beautiful and I feel free. The sky within me is as wide as the one stretching above my head.

Etty worked for the Jewish Council in Amsterdam, an organisation formed by the Germans as a go-between of Jews and the occupying forces. This role prolonged her life as Etty, initially, was not sent to Westerbork. This was a transit camp comprising of a half kilometre patch of overcrowding and misery where Jews from the Netherlands as well as further afield were incarcerated before being herded onto trains heading East. And although she most certainly knew where her fate lay, she records in great detail how she refuses to give into fear and hate. Etty constantly resisted attempts by her friends in Amsterdam to convince her to go into hiding, so great was her need to live open-heartedly through those terrible times and extend compassion to those around her. Before she is sent to Westerbork, she writes that *I would like to feel the contours of these times with my fingertips*. By tapping into the source of a rich inner life, she wants to be in the midst of suffering so she can be the *thinking heart of the barracks*. Inconceivable to us, perhaps, that she chose to not give herself a chance of life but, instead, reach out to others at Westerbork. *I want to be right there in the thick of what people call 'horror' and still be able to say: Life is beautiful*, she writes.

At the transit camp, she nursed the sick in the hospital barracks and listened compassionately to those who wanted to talk. People remembered her for always having a kind word for others; for being a shining beacon in a time of immeasurable darkness. Etty was sent to the gas chambers in 1943 in Auschwitz and left behind her a remarkable legacy, for reading her words are to be struck on each new page how fresh and relevant they remain; how deeply compassionate and self-compassionate they are. *Sometimes the most important thing in a whole day*, wrote Etty, *is the rest we take between two deep breaths, or the turning inwards in prayer for five short minutes*. So much wisdom rests in those simple words; I feel as though I have spent a summer in the company of a remarkable new friend and I know that the spirit of Etty will always remain with me.

About half-way through our French road trip, we stop for the night at an *aire* in a clearing of trees, one of the thousands of free parking sites that France is so renowned for. Living in such close proximity to Andy and our three children, there have been many times over the course of this journey that I have had to take myself off on my own so I can really release the tears that need to come. On this occasion, our motorhome is parked above a densely forested, rocky ravine. I move away swiftly and soundlessly from my family and step one foot after the other as I find a place to be alone. Sitting on a rocky outcrop, the evening sun is dipping and I hug my knees to my chest and sob. I am there for some time before I hear a rustle behind me. Looking back, I see that my eldest daughter has appeared. Wiping at my eyes, I try to pull myself upwards and appear as though I have it together as I don't

The Sky Within Rebecca Stonehill

want her to see me like this. But it cannot work of course; the mere effort of trying to look strong only results in the tears coursing through my body more violently.

My daughter approaches and crouches down beside me. She is not demonstrative by nature, a quiet, calm and, by turn, calming soul. But she reaches out a hand and presses it into my shoulder. She makes gentle murmurs of compassion as the sun continues its descent and I cry and cry, but these tears are not the straightforward tears of grief for my lost self; they are also tears of thankfulness for the life and words of Etty Hillesum and, particularly at that moment, a deep gratitude for my daughter who feels comfortable enough to just sit with me in my sorrow.

I used to worry a great deal about how my situation must be impacting on my family, my fear for them and what they 'should' or 'shouldn't' witness far eclipsing any self-compassion I had for myself. I believed that my sadness must be negatively affecting them all, particularly my three children who are at tender ages of discovery and growth. Whilst that early evening with my daughter in France felt beautiful and nurturing, it came with it a prickling of discomfort that wouldn't go away; if that sensation could have spoken, it would have said, This is all wrong. This is the wrong way around – you are meant to be strong for your children.

As time has passed, I have come to recognise that the light punctuating the darkness compensates for this. In fact, it more than compensates, the light cannot be without the dark. By showing my children that I am an imperfect and vulnerable being I am, I hope, being my truest self and not suppressing my sadness in order to protect them. There is a balance, naturally, to be sought here. But I am still learning to be kind to myself and celebrate moments of joy, beauty and courage in often unexpected places, as well as embracing my frailties. Brené Brown expresses this perfectly: *I want our home to be a place where we can be our bravest selves and our most fearful selves.* Compassion for myself continues to grow and I think now with a degree of disbelief about the hard time I used to give myself; the harsh volley of inner criticism that I meted out upon an already bruised soul. *Can you be a little bit of a better friend to yourself?* asks Elizabeth Gilbert. *Would you ever allow a friend to speak of themselves the way you do in your interior moments?* It is a work in progress, a slow, steady work of patience and self-compassion.

The root of the word compassion comes from the latin, *compati*, which means 'to suffer with.' For a long time, I don't think I truly grasped the distinction between kindness and compassion, and while kindness is a vital ingredient of life, compassion does something different: it brings presence to the suffering of other people or to ourselves.

In Hinduism, Buddhism and Jainism, compassion is known as *karuna*. This is derived from the Sanskrit word *kara* which means 'to do' or 'to make.' This means that being compassionate is active; its essence is physical. And it's not just about practising compassion with others – we must also be compassionate towards ourselves. One really cannot work without the other. In other words, we can only be truly compassionate towards others if we can first root that in ourselves.

In both Hebrew and Arabic, the root of the word for compassion comes from 'womb', the interweaving of physicality and love. New life in these traditions can be framed through words and deeds, with compassion helping us to embrace deep respect and tenderness for life. This is not just the life of others; we must remember our own lives. I, like most people, am pretty good at being compassionate to others, but on the whole, I find it far less easy to extend this sentiment towards myself. And yet, like a muscle that needs exercising, I must cultivate this as a starting point and springboard for everything else that happens in my life. But what does self-compassion look like?

Self-compassion can come in many forms. It is tuning in and asking myself what I need in a certain moment. It is non-judgmental and often manifests in calm, quiet ways. Self-compassion can be gifting to myself time for a walk, even when I don't feel like going, and noticing small things around me: the buds of new wildflowers coming out or the slant of sunlight on the path in front of me. Self-compassion can be wrapping arms around myself and giving myself a long, deep hug if there is nobody there to hug me. Touch is so important. It is an act of self-love and self-acceptance. Francis Weller writes that *self-compassion is not an event, but an ongoing, daily practice. It is the root practice for our inner life and also for our relational lives.*

Another useful metaphor is Tara Brach's two wings of seeing clearly what is going on (mindfulness) and holding our experience with compassion (heartfulness). In other words, these two interdependent wings encompass open and unconditional awareness of what is arising within us and being tender with this. Just sitting with it and holding it. I love the imagery of this, that we need both of these wings together in order to be able to fly. It is interesting to note that in a number of Asian languages, the words for mind

The Sky Within Rebecca Stonehill

and heart are actually the same. While we may consider mindfulness to be solely about paying attention, some cultures instinctively know that this is so deeply interwoven with a tender compassion that the two are inseparable. *Whenever we feel closed down, hurt or unforgiving,* Tara Brach says, *by simply breathing in and gently touching the rawness of our pain, we can begin to transform our suffering into compassion.*

When a person is struggling with chronic insomnia, people always have suggestions to try and alleviate it, because everybody sleeps. And everybody knows what it is to sleep poorly on occasion. Conversely, if someone has, let's say, a challenging skin condition for example, there probably won't be as many suggestions because far less people can claim to know how that feels. Suggestions that have come my way over the years have ranged from the simple herbal teas and lavender oils in the bath through to complimentary therapies and online sleep courses. These people mean well, of course they do, and they only want to see me well. But because chronic insomnia is not a 'quantifiable' illness in the same way that other conditions are, it can often end up being far lonelier, just as conditions of mental health often are. Also, the right to offer unsolicited advice is placed far more firmly in the public realm. There is a common assumption that I would like advice, even if I haven't asked for it. But this condition, though far less tangible and with wide-ranging roots, is very real. It can last for several nights or it can last for decades. But it is real. It may not be able to kill us, but it can slowly and painfully erode our self-esteem, our *joie de vivre*, the very fabric of our souls. The part of the brain that regulates emotions, the amygdala, doesn't function well after a sleepless night. Whereas people generally catch up with the odd bad night and their emotions are able to settle, compounded nights of sleeplessness can wreak havoc on the amygdala and one's ability to relate to others.

People sometimes ask me what it actually feels like. How to describe it? Wading through treacle in painfully slow motion; hearing people speak and understanding the words but not being able to connect them; a world in 2D cardboard, flat and drained of colour and contrast; the headache at the temples that won't go away; the tears that won't stop. It is completely brutal.

For many years, I would take up those nuggets of suggestions that people laid down for me as a matter of duty. Was this something I had not already tried? If so, I owed it to myself and the friend who suggested it to give it a go. But because there were so many suggestions coming my way due to our common human need to sleep, over time this created overwhelm and anxiety, which subsequently fed into the loop of poor sleep. What was wrong with me, my mind asked, if I was trying all these things that have worked for so many others, and I still wasn't sleeping?

As the years have passed, I have become much better at telling people what I need. Or what I don't need. I owe it to myself to find a non-critical way to thank people for thinking of me, but I am not looking for suggestions because I am taking my own steps with this. I, and those very closest people to me, know best which way I need to proceed. This may be infuriating to some people, insulting even to others when they are trying to help me. But it feels important I stand my ground with this. It's important that I show myself compassion on this journey.

Once we begin to offer more self-compassion to ourselves, perhaps we will slowly notice that our confidence in who we are and what we need will also naturally grow. I also have an unformed sense that my experiences will one day, somehow, be able to help other people. Perhaps it will be through these words I'm writing right now; perhaps it will be through physically speaking to others who have been through something similar. I don't know how it will all progress, but I wear this belief like a loose, undefined second skin. In the words of Rachel Naomi Remen, *often we connect through our wounds, through the wisdom we have gained, the growth that has happened to us. Because we have been wounded allows us to be of help to other people.*

It seems easy enough to be kind and compassionate, a good listener and good friend when I am feeling bright and all is well with the world. But when we are feeling great sorrow, the last thing we feel able to do is reach out to others in their own plights. Of course some issues are more serious than others, but it's not a competition. There is no sliding scale of suffering. I love how Brené Brown frames it: *I've… learned that the more we diminish our own pain, or rank it compared to what others have survived, the less empathic we are to everyone.*

During those times when I am at my lowest, I may feel incapable of assisting and being there for others; it is often not practical, nor possible. But at the same time there are small, even tiny things that reach across the gulf, extending a hand of compassion to others in their struggles. Rachel Naomi Remen, who has struggled with debilitating Crohn's Disease for many years, says that *my own wounds, my own sufferings, have enabled me to feel compassion for the sufferings of others. Without my suffering, I wouldn't understand the suffering of others or be able to connect to them. My loneliness enables me to recognize the loneliness in other*

The Sky Within Rebecca Stonehill

people, even when it's covered over; to find them where they have become lost in the dark, and sit with them; and to know that just by sitting with them, eventually they will find what they need in order to move forward.

How would it be if we were to believe that our own suffering could help relieve the pain of another? That without the suffering we have experienced ourselves we would not be able to respond to others in the way they need to be heard? As Rachel Naomi Remen suggests, often words are not even needed. Sometimes, sitting with another and being present for them can be the most powerful gift of all. *People will say,* Remen says, *well, how can I make a difference when I'm so wounded, myself? How can I make a difference when I feel so not-enough? But it's our very wounds that enable us to make a difference. We are the right people, just as we are.*

When my heart is broken open with the sorrow I experience, I am also being offered one of the greatest gifts of humanity: the ability to feel the suffering of others. From her beautiful poem, *Kindness*, Naomi Nye explores this idea:

'Before you know kindness as the deepest thing inside,
you must know sorrow as the other deepest thing.
You must wake up with sorrow.
You must speak it till your voice
catches the thread of all sorrows
and you see the size of the cloth.'

When I suffer, I am learning how to be there for others, how to be what psychoanalyst Carl Jung describes as a 'wounded healer.' Even sitting with the possibility of that, even if it doesn't feel quite true right now, is profound. One day, perhaps someone will need me in their own pain and what I am going through is paving the way for me to be there for them. Because as I have learnt, what I need more than anything is presence to what I am going through. I cannot be 'fixed' by others, but they can tenderly and compassionately care for me, and that is what I will be able to one day pass on to another. *We help some time pass for those suffering,* says writer Anne Lamott. *We sit with them in their hopeless pain and feel terrible with them, without trying to fix them with platitudes; doing this with them is just about the most gracious gift we have to offer.*

A wonderful example of this is looking at the life of Anthony Ray Hinton. When I discovered his autobiography, *The Sun Does Shine*, I read it from cover to cover, hardly looking up. Anthony Ray Hinton, most commonly known as 'Ray' is from Alabama, USA. At the age of twenty-nine, he was convicted of the two murders of restaurant managers and, following a prejudiced trial in which key evidence was ignored (for example – that at the time of one of the murders, he was working a night shift on the other side of town), he was sent to Death Row. When he was arrested, the police told him in no uncertain terms that he would be going to jail because he was black. Ray was what I'd describe as a 'loveable rogue' – he'd had brushes with the law before but had never hurt a soul. He was deeply devoted to his mother, loved his community and his church, was a talented baseball player and had a tendency to turn the ladies' eye.

'Innocent' was written all over his case, but Ray was a scapegoat, deemed a criminal because he was born poor and black in the wrong place. Alabama was a state where the Klu Klux Klan roamed freely and racist hate crimes were commonplace. An old pistol was found in his mother's home that the experts agreed had not been fired in twenty-seven years. And yet, despite overwhelming evidence that should rightfully have sent him home, he was incarcerated in the living hell of Alabama's Death Row where he, like the other inmates, was kept in solitary confinement, was stripped of all human rights and where his grief and bitterness at what had happened to him festered like an open wound.

Ray refused to open his mouth to talk to the wardens or other prisoners. The sole light in his life was the weekly visits, for a single hour, of his closest friend who made a seven-hour round trip every week to see him, and less frequently his beloved mother, who found the long journey gruelling. Every time his attorney appealed against his conviction, it was quashed and legal loopholes ensured he was kept behind bars.

A broken man, every day Ray had to listen to the tormented cries of his fellow inmates, awaiting their deaths. He also had to endure, many times, the smell of burnt flesh from the death chamber just thirty feet from his cell. The passage that had the deepest impact on me in his autobiography was an event that occurred three years into his incarceration. He was listening to the anguished sobbing of another inmate nearby throughout the night. He tried to ignore the sound, pacing constantly up and down his small cell to take his mind off it. But the sobbing escalated and showed no sign of abating. Something in Ray snapped, but rather than the words angrily gushing from his mouth that he expected, he took himself entirely by surprise as he heard himself calling out into the darkness *Are you ok?*

The Sky Within Rebecca Stonehill

Breaking three years of silence on Death Row, what went on to take place is nothing short of extraordinary. Ray learnt that his fellow inmate had just found out his mother had died. Over the next two hours, Ray coaxed stories out of him about his mother and his home life, humanising a deeply de-humanising environment. And it didn't stop there – from that point on, Ray realised that he had a choice: to drown in his own bitterness or to bring some light into the dark lives of those around him. He chose the latter. *You didn't have to be on death row to feel all alone,* he writes in his book, *and I know there were people all over the world, at this exact moment, sitting on the edge of their beds and crying.* He helped other prisoners to become aware of their rights and formed a Death Row Book Club, in order to give people *an hour away from the rats and the roaches and the smell of death and decay.* Not unlike Etty Hillesum at Westerbork, he became known on the Row as the man whom others approached to seek some solace. *There is a point in a struggle when you have to surrender,* he writes. *You have to stop trying to swim upstream, fighting the current.* Whilst in prison, he watched fifty-three men and one woman walk past his cell on their way to the execution chamber. He got everyone on Death Row to bang on the bars of their cell five minutes before the inmates were executed. *We were banging the bars,* he says, *to say to those who were being put to death, we're with you, we still love you right up to the end.*

Ray was eventually granted freedom. He never received an apology from the state of Alabama for having thirty years of his life taken from him. But through extraordinary humanity, he chose to forgive those who had wronged him. If he didn't take that path, he said that he would have remained imprisoned. When he was interviewed on the US television show *Sixty Minutes* following his release, his interviewer was incredulous when Anthony said that he had forgiven those who had sent him to jail. *If I'm angry and unforgiving,* he said, *they will have taken the rest of my life.* Ray now spends his time as a sought-after public speaker, delivering messages of a flawed criminal justice system, faith, hope and forgiveness.

When reaching out to others is absolutely the last thing I feel capable of doing, this could be the time that presents the most growth if I can reach beyond that. We are hard-wired to be compassionate, and when we don't respond to that fundamental law of our being, we will feel it in some way. The Dalai Lama puts it this way: *...when you say 'How can I help?' even in the midst of your deep anguish, it's got an alchemy that transforms your pain. It may not take it away. But it becomes in a way bearable...*

So my sorrows shape and mould me and are gifting me the ability, and everyone else who suffers, to be compassionate, and in our broken world there is no greater need. *This is who I think we are supposed to be,* says Anne Lamott, *people who help call forth human beings from deep inside hopelessness.* It may not be possible now. It may not be possible until years down the line, but when the time is right, we will be the greatest wounded healers of them all.

The Sky Within Rebecca Stonehill

The Spaciousness of Uncertainty

'In addition to a sense of humour, a basic support for a joyful mind is curiosity, paying attention, taking an interest in the world around you. You don't actually have to be happy. But being curious without a heavy judgmental attitude helps. If you are judgmental, you can even be curious about that.'

Pema Chödrön

Not long after sitting inside an A&E hospital room with Andy, I find myself on a plane to Zürich. The night that had led me to the emergency room had been building for a long time, and we knew we couldn't ignore it anymore: I wasn't going to just 'get better' on my own without intervention and support. Over the years, I have taken more anti-depressants and sleeping pills than I care to remember, often a heady cocktail of the two. Now, I must confront the reality that they are not working; if anything, they are making everything far, far more difficult.

Along with one of my close friends, the godmother of my daughter, and Andy search high and low for a holistic residential clinic. I have been to see so, so many people over the years, but these people have not been under one roof; they have not been working together to look at the whole person. We are bewildered to find that nothing that seems to fit the bill can be found in England. There are plenty of sleep clinics or sleep 'spas', but this isn't what we're looking for. We want a scientific, thorough examination of my blood, my hormones, my spit, my shit, all of it. And I don't want to be medicated anymore. I don't want to go to a place where a possible outcome is to tweak the anti-depressants. And so we settle on a Biological Medicine clinic of diagnostics and therapeutics in the mountains an hour from Zürich and I make my way out there to spend a month away from my family. It costs a fortune – we take deep breaths and spill out the coffers of our savings and remind ourselves that we don't need the latest gadgets or fancy holidays. In fact, we don't need holidays at all – that's why we have the motorhome, even

The Sky Within Rebecca Stonehill

if the paintwork is peeling and the windows keep falling in. What we need is a workable family life.

It feels huge. I've spent a few weeks apart from Andy before when he's been away with work trips, but the longest I've spent away from my kids has been a week. My son and middle daughter won't talk about it. Whenever I've queried them if they want to ask me any questions, they look at me, shrug and then shake their heads. As for my eldest child, although she also doesn't have any specific questions about my condition because instinctively, I know she understands, she is interested in knowing what kind of treatments they'll give me once there. I'm interested too. I've spent some time poring over their website and speaking to one of the doctor's there, but it's not going to make real sense until I actually arrive.

I take a sleeping pill for reassurance and travel to Zürich one evening in January. The flight arrives late and I take a train to a small, sleepy village where it seems so improbable to me that a cutting-edge clinic exists. As I wheel my bag up a steep hill towards the AirBnB I am to be staying in close to the clinic, snowflakes start to gently float down around me. I stop and look up into the black sky, now punctuated with white, whirling forms. I can't remember the last time I've seen snow – it's been years. We only returned from living in Nairobi a year and a half ago and Norfolk, where we're now living, is renowned for being one of the UK's driest counties. I close my eyes as I allow the snow to settle on my face and think of my children. How they would love to see this. How they long for snow.

My AirBnB is a wonderful, airy studio built into the side of a modern, wooden chalet with breathtaking views of the mountains. The hosts are friendly and charming, clearly curious that I have come to spend time at the clinic but not fishing for any further information. I unpack my bags, peer out of the window one last time as the snow silently falls, then close the curtains. And then, a curious thing happens. I don't take a sleeping aid, and I go to bed. And I sleep.

I also sleep the next night, and the one after that. And that is before there have been any interventions. Even with all the treatments in place, the curious thing is that I continue to sleep well, on the whole, for the entire duration of my stay in Switzerland. I speak to my family almost daily and continue to read my children a night-time story, narrating the pages of *Watership Down* into the recording device on *WhatsApp*. They are not small children anymore, but it's a habit we've never lost and it helps me to still feel a part of their everyday lives. The irony is not lost on any of us that here I am in a different country, finally with some energy, and nobody to socialise with or share this new lease of life with.

I go through all the lab diagnostics and the doctors and practitioners there are kind, compassionate, professional. My days are a whirlwind of intensive treatments; I am given infusions of iron, vitamins and minerals; I have amalgam fillings removed as the mercury in them can cause a myriad of health problems.; I work with a coach who gives me advice on calming the autonomic nervous system; I am put on a programme of supplements; review my diet with a nutritionist and have various cutting-edge therapies, most of which I've never even heard of. I am given a book to read about Highly Sensitive People (HSP's) and strongly identify with the traits described. Astonished that I have never heard this term before, I am fitted for a mouth guard to help reduce my incessant nightly teeth grinding, a common habit amongst HSP's.

I'd like to pause here briefly to explore HSP's because even now as I write this, I can't believe how few people are familiar with this common character trait (believed by Dr Elaine Aron who wrote the first of many books on HSP's to encompass up to 20% of the global population) or why it is not in the lexicon of doctors, of teachers, of parents. There is also still such a stigma associated with sensitivity. *Don't be so over-sensitive!* You may have heard that one before and, if not directed at you, at somebody you know. There are so many examples I could use, but let me give you just a few to demonstrate how this plays out in my own life. Even when I was much younger, in my late teens and twenties when I used to love going out with friends to nightclubs or busy bars, there would always be several points during the evening when I would find myself retreating to a quiet space alone outside or locking myself into toilet cubicles. I didn't understand why; I was having a good time, but it never felt like an option not to do this. To be honest, I just thought I was a little odd but didn't think too much about it.

More recently, Andy would sometimes be talking to me but I could see frustration cloud his face and he commented that I wasn't really listening to him. I am, I would say, I'm trying to. Again, I couldn't understand why I was not able to focus on him and his words, leading to numerous frustrating interactions. Now, with the knowledge of high sensitivity firmly in my awareness, I realise that with both scenarios I had gone into overwhelm mode. In the nightclubs, my finely tuned nervous system couldn't cope with all the noise, smells, bright lights and crowds and I had to take time out.

The Sky Within Rebecca Stonehill

With my conversations with Andy (or anyone else), it could be as simple as the fact that I couldn't focus on his words because the radio was playing in the background, or my children were having a conversation nearby. It's like all my synapses were firing and I was quickly pushed into overwhelm. Now I can recognise when I am in this situation and switch the radio off or stop him very quickly and say, I can't have this conversation here, can we go to another room? Just as I know that if I am in a supermarket or shopping mall (two of the most triggering places for HSP's), it helps hugely to walk around with headphones on listening to calm music or words. Even then, I often find once I have returned home from these kinds of places that I need to lie down briefly in a quiet, dark room. This is simply the way it is for me and hundreds of thousands of others across the globe, the majority of whom are not aware of this innate character trait and suffer needlessly. If all of this sounds extreme, a plethora of research has been undertaken and published on HSP's. It's a fast-growing area of study and I've included a few suggestions for starting points in the resources section at the end of the book.

Back in Switzerland, when I have a little time off, I put my walking boots on and stride into the mountains. I even meet up with two sets of friends who also live in the German-speaking part of the country as well as my half-sister who lives in the French part. Being here feels indulgent, nurturing and spacious. I am being taken seriously. It feels like a relief. But the niggle never leaves me: why can't I sleep like this when I'm back home? I don't have a stressful life; there is no reason for me not to be sleeping at home. It is just so deeply habitual, and some habits are harder to break than others. I feel nervous when my month draws to a close and high winds mean that my flight is postponed and I wonder ironically if this is a sign, though I don't know for what. But the following day, the winds die down and I fly back to England. I am overjoyed to see my family again and they too, are happy to have me home. This mother and wife is a bouncier, happier version of the one who left for Zürich a month previously and when people ask me if I think the effects of my time there will have a lasting impact, I don't miss a beat: definitely, I say. Of course there will be ups and downs still, but I'm much, much better.

And the truth is that I am much better for some time. I can't quite believe it – it feels nothing short of a miracle – but for the first three months after I return home I sleep as though I'm in a coma. I haven't slept this well for years. I wake up not being able to get over the fact that I can smile in the morning, that I have energy and enthusiasm for the day ahead of me.

The unravelling of all this is a slow burn: the odd night here and there and I cheerfully grin and shrug it off. Of course I'm going to have a honeymoon period, I tell myself and others. It's not possible – or even desirable – to stay on this kind of high long-term. Fast forward several months and my smile is a little more strained but I'm still hanging in there. I'm practising everything I learnt at the clinic, I am taking the supplements, I am travelling to London once a month for intravenous infusions of iron as well as vitamins and minerals and I am following my nutrition plan. I am definitely in denial for some time that my sleep is slipping and I cling onto it like a drowning person clinging on to a lifebuoy. It does stay however, more or less manageable for some time, even with the highs and lows. Because I have learnt, haven't I, that we can't even access the sweetness of those energetic days without knowing how it feels to be floundering in the depths. The weighing scales manage to just about balance out so that I can maintain some equilibrium. I can make plans, I can do things, albeit in a very restricted Covid kind-of-way. I speak to a couple of the doctors and therapists I had a good rapport with from the Swiss clinic and they reassure me this is completely normal. I nod my head and agree and I get on with living my life.

I keep coping. Until I realise that I'm not coping anymore and the grief of this floors me. Just as the UK emerges from a long, strict, difficult lockdown in the wake of the Covid pandemic, blinking groggily into the spring sunshine, I am drawing the curtains again to block out the light. Around this time, I read popular American author Elizabeth Gilbert's words on grief, who lost her partner to pancreatic and liver cancer:

Grief...happens upon you, it's bigger than you. There is a humility that you have to step into, when you surrender to being moved through the landscape of grief by grief itself. And it has its own time-frame, it has its own itinerary with you, it has its own power over you, and it will come when it comes. And when it comes, it's a bow-down. It's a carve out. And it comes when it wants to, and it carves you out – it comes in the middle of the night, comes in the middle of the day, comes in the middle of a meeting, comes in the middle of a meal. It arrives – it's this tremendously forceful arrival and it cannot be resisted without you suffering more...

While my situation could not be more different from Elizabeth Gilbert's, I am grieving a loss: the loss of myself. The re-loss of myself. And yes, it's a carve out. As the weeks roll by, I start to cynically wonder if Switzerland was just a very expensive way to get some time on my own and to confirm what wasn't wrong with me. But as I breathe deeply into my sorrow, I notice something interesting has happened. I notice that some things have changed, some very important things. It takes a while to realise, but when I do, it takes me by surprise:

I no longer feel guilty about being a bad mother or a bad wife, because I no longer believe I am either of those things. I am simply a woman who is having a hard time. I also have more clarity now about what I need and letting go of expectations upon myself. I am, in short, far, far kinder to myself than I used to be. I have stopped apologising to people and taken far more care with that oft-used word, sorry. Why do we feel the need to incessantly apologise when we have done nothing wrong? Should I be sorry for being unwell? For suffering? What I have learnt is that, over time, the more we apologise for what we should not be sorry for, the more this chips away at our hearts and souls and erodes our self-esteem. Of course we should apologise when we have wronged somebody, but this is not what I am talking about. We must stop saying sorry for things that are beyond our control; for our frailties. We must claim them as part of the intricate and complex web of human vulnerabilities. This is not a situation I ever imagined myself to be in, but this is where I am. I remember only too well the times when I used to say, over and again, during my hardest times, this is not a life. This is not living. And now? It may not be the life I envisaged for myself, but it most definitely is a life. In all its brokenness, I am living.

Whilst the effects of my time in Switzerland are not immediately obvious (save for the miraculous buoyant 'honeymoon' that characterises the first few months back home), the book that one of the clinic's therapists placed in my hands about HSP's couldn't have been more important. It's never going to be a quick fix to really learn about and understand this trait, and to then implement my findings into my own daily life. It's also not just coincidence that I am away from my family and I am sleeping. Yes, it is true that on many occasions I have been alone and still not slept. And I love them deeply and want to be with Andy and my three children, but clearly, something about the longevity of this time away answered a call in me, to really devote time to myself, no easy task when this can often be viewed as navel gazing at best and woefully self-indulgent at worst. But I must shut off these perceptions of what others may or may not think. At the end of the day, this isn't important at all. What is important is to understand what I really need. There's no easy answer to this, particularly if spending almost a month away from my family (certainly not a long-term solution) seems to alleviate my sleeplessness. More than anything at this juncture, I must remain curious.

I have learnt that one of the ways to move through the slipstream of my suffering is to remain curious about my experiences; to ask myself Where am I at? Where am I feeling this emotion? What is happening in my body? What more can I learn? Curiosity is an interesting trait, as for most of humanity's time on earth, it has courted stories of warning. Negative connotations have abounded of curiosity being akin to meddling, undoubtedly bolstered from the early stories of Adam and Eve and the apple of knowledge, Icarus flying too close to the sun and the events that befell Pandora when she opened the box.

Curiosity, however, has now evolved and blossomed into a far more desirable quality. We all know that to be curious is a wondrous thing in life. It keeps our eyes open to the world unfolding around us and helps us to appreciate, with child-like awe, what we have around and within us. Curiosity helped Alice to embrace the adventures that lay in her path down the rabbit hole, but it also killed the cat. And sometimes, when we are in the midst of our suffering, this emotion is the last thing we feel willing or able to conjure up. And yet, curiosity could just be our saving grace during difficult times. It is normal to want to know why things are a certain way and to find answers. After all, knowledge is power, isn't it? In some ways, if we use it the right way, it can be. And yet, we could be missing a more subtle part of the equation. According to Maria Kalman, a celebrated American artist working at the intersection of art and philosophy: *you don't really have to have knowledge — what you have to have is curiosity.*

It is impossible to be able to put everything we do and experience into neat little boxes with labels on them, and certainly not the transitoriness of human nature. As Pema Chödrön says, *we can be suffering and be curious about our suffering at the same time, though the two may not initially feel compatible. Being curious is essentially a profound paying attention to what is taking place both within and without. It is seeking and it is asking questions and yet, herein lies the key: curiosity does not ask for a definitive answer. The most important thing is to look at our feelings with gentle interest rather than self-judgment or rejection. It is about meeting each person, event and feeling that arises in our lives with an abiding sense of curiosity so that rather than stepping down those well-trodden routes of habitual reactivity, we can try to steer ourselves in a direction of quietly and patiently noticing.*

Rainer Maria Rilke, poet and novelist, talked about the importance of asking questions, a fertile breeding ground for the gains that can be ours in the face of curiosity: *don't search for the answers, which could not be given to you now, because you would not be able to live them. And the point it to live everything. Live the questions now. Perhaps then, someday far in the future, you will gradually, without even*

The Sky Within Rebecca Stonehill

noticing it, live your way into the answer.

But how to live the questions? As I mentioned earlier, one possible answer to this lies in embodiment, which essentially points to our bodily experience and reactions to situations. In other words, when I start paying attention to what is happening in my body – when I'm stressed, when I'm angry or sad, when I'm standing at the checkout line at the supermarket or when I'm feeling supremely relaxed, reactions are taking place in my body. It could be that my breathing is shallow or that I'm biting my bottom lip. Perhaps there is a tightness across my chest and, if I dig a little deeper, I realise that I am feeling afraid. Once I begin to recognise these sensations for what they are, I can bring a curiosity to them and, for example, a softness to the fear so that I am no longer controlled by it but, rather, I can move towards a kind response to my own experiences.

I want to be clear here: being curious does not mean that I don't do anything. It is not characterised by inaction. Author Rebecca Solnit writes that *hope locates itself in the premises that we don't know what will happen and that in the spaciousness of uncertainty is room to act.* There is always room to act. But through retaining a gentle curiosity, rather than being reactive, I can learn to live from a place of embodied wisdom and integrity. It is curiosity that has led me to be a writer. As a young girl, I would squeeze myself into the branches of a tree, cupboards or under beds with a notebook and pencil, observing the intricate dance of nature, people coming and going and conversations before scribbling down ideas for possible stories or poems. I am so interested in people, our interactions and the words spoken and left unspoken. Perhaps it is curiosity that has led to my issues with sleep, because I take everything in and I feel things very deeply. But being curious about my life and the wider ripples this may bring also feels key.

I don't pretend to have all the answers. I still fall apart, completely and utterly. But I know that I will never stop being curious, about the world around me, about other people and about my own experience. Perhaps, as Rilke says, one day my curiosity will enable me to live my way into the answer. And the question? What my unique footprint on this planet means.

Day and Night Gifts

'It is not happiness that makes us grateful, it is gratefulness that makes us happy. If you think it's happiness that makes us grateful, think again.'

Brother David Steindl-Rast, Catholic Benedictine Monk, Author & Lecturer

I am taking one of those solo trips I am coming to know so well, a time when – for reasons unknown – the possibility of rest opens up to me. This time, Andy has driven me in our motorhome to a remote spot on the North Norfolk coast in June called Buttercup Meadow where I am to spend four days. There is a smattering of other motorhomes here, no electrical hookup, no shower block and it is about a five minute walk from a sandy beach.

Andy, consistently supportive, consistently kind, brings his bike in the motorhome so that he can cycle to the nearest train station to get back to Norwich. As I watch his curly head disappear around the corner, I stand outside the motorhome and take a deep breath. Here I am again. The truth is that I don't always sleep when I come away on my own, but often I do, even if it's just for the first night or two. It seems that being away from all responsibilities triggers a relaxation response and working to my own timetable (eating when I'm hungry, going for a walk where I want, when I want, not having to think about packed lunches and children's activities) answers a call in me.

Andy and I met and married relatively young (by today's standards). We were both doing voluntary work in Guatemala when I met him on a bus in a small town on the shores of Atitlán, a verdant lake fringed with volcanoes and hillside villages. He was from a town just half an hour away from where I lived back in England and was one of the only Britts I met during my six months in Guatemala. We talked for two hours as our 'chicken bus' (as the local transportation is known, carrying its cargo of humans, goats and, of course, chickens) careered around the lake, barely drawing breath. I had to

The Sky Within Rebecca Stonehill

get off before him and I reluctantly bade him farewell. Just before I climbed down from the bus, something made me dash back before it resumed its frenzied course and I asked for his email address. Clutching the precious scrap of paper, I rushed off the bus and stood on the roadside with my backpack, dust whirling in its wake as we both raised our hands. It had only been two hours, but I knew I would see him again.

This 'again' came a month or so later, when we met to climb Santa Maria Volcano during full moon, starting our hike late at night with a group and tour guide and reaching the summit as the sun was rising and a smaller active volcano nearby was erupting, plumes of grey smoke billowing out of the top like organ bellows. We were smitten with one another and it was all wonderful, exhilarating, life-affirming. We were engaged by the end of the year back in England and our eldest daughter came hot off the press. He was, and still is, a person to trust with my life: kind, creative, passionate, capable, adventurous. I'd hardly had time to get used to him, let alone a baby, but of course all of that didn't register at the time; it's only with the benefit of hindsight it takes on a different resonance. Becoming a wife and then mother in close succession, at a time when only a single one of my friends had experienced motherhood, felt at the time…I don't know, daring? I look back on it now and it's clear how dramatically my life changed in such a short space of time. I made the choice of course, and while I wouldn't wish things to be another way, everything changed so quickly; there I was doing my own thing, passionately independent, but suddenly (at least, it seems sudden now), by the age of twenty-eight I was a married mother.

When Andy cycles away from the motorhome, I feel nothing but gratitude. Yes, I am having a hard time which is what has led me to this solitary, windswept meadow on the North Norfolk coast. But look what I have. Look who crossed my path all those years ago. Look what we have, despite the difficult times. And look at the beauty of this place I find myself in now. I walk around the meadow, watching birds being carried in squalls of wind buffeting around me, the sun shining in my face. And I pick a few wildflowers, making sure there are enough of them around to do so. Back at the motorhome, I boil water for tea and as I wait, I take out a tiny vase from one of the cupboards and slip the few stems of wildflowers in it and place it on the table. Such a small, simple act but looking at them makes me inordinately happy.

Sorrow and gratitude are not two words that we would normally put together. When the edge of my reality is blurred with grief, how can I open to gratitude? How can I find that space inside that helps me to appreciate the beauty of life and what it has to offer? I have learnt over the years that gratitude is a perfect practice for when I am feeling low. It can help me to focus on what is good in my life – and I can always find something. Always. Human nature dictates a bias towards negativity; in other words, we tend to think of or recall what is going wrong more easily than what is going right. This takes practice to tip the balance scales the other way, but it is an important, gentle nudge that opens our hearts to what we still do have when we feel like very little is working in our lives.

David Whyte expresses it beautifully, that gratitude is the recognition ...*that we are miraculously part of something, rather than nothing. Even if that something is temporarily pain or despair, we inhabit a living world, with real faces, real voices, laughter, the colour blue, the green of the fields, the freshness of a cold wind, or the tawny hue of a winter landscape.* It may be true that it is easy to feel grateful for what I have when all is well; when I see the world through the glass half-full lens rather than half-empty. But Kristi Nelson, Director of *A Network for Grateful Living* talks about the significance of simply being in possession of a glass: *it seems to me that underneath all the inevitable risings and fallings, feeling deeply content or joyful is not actually about how full the glass is or seems...it is about being grateful for having a glass at all...the glass is a container for our experiences – all experience – and some people seem to know that noticing and being grateful for this container dwarfs everything, and can turn any and all contents in our favour.*

But what about when I feel truly awful? When I feel utterly incapable of conjuring up this sentiment? Robert Emmons is a psychologist and a leading scientific expert on gratitude who has extensively studied why gratitude matters and how it can be cultivated. He believes that if we can keep an attitude of gratitude to flourish in the midst of suffering and difficulties, this is what will make the true difference to our lives. *It is precisely under crisis conditions,* he writes, *when we have the most to gain by a grateful perspective on life.* He encourages us to *move forward in a posture of hope and possibility. So gratitude becomes part of the coping, healing process.*

None of this is easy; in fact, it is quite the opposite. If we are struggling with illness or bereavement or unemployment or a whole raft of other things (or, in my case, if I am feeling overwhelmed by emotion when I haven't slept well for days on end), we cannot 'make' ourselves feel grateful or more happy. But this is not about denying the pain we are going through; in fact, during dark days, when people urge us to 'count our blessings', it can have quite the adverse affect and cause us further distress. When I first started

The Sky Within Rebecca Stonehill

consciously engaging with gratitude, I remember on many occasions feeling like it wasn't going to work. For how could I possibly be grateful when I felt so low that I sometimes simply wanted to disappear? Or start up a gratitude journal when actually, that felt like a smack in the face or, at least, a glib papering over or suppression of reality?

David Steindl-Rast is a Benedictine monk and author who has studied Gratitude for decades, writing and lecturing on it extensively. He explains it this way: *on the personal level, we cannot be grateful for the loss of a friend, for unfaithfulness, for bereavement... but we can be grateful in every given moment; for the opportunity. And even when we are confronted with something that is terribly difficult, we can rise to this occasion and respond to this opportunity that is given to us.*

I do believe now that an unforeseen opportunity lies in my experiences; there is a gift in what I am going through that I may not be able to see now. In fact, I may not understand it for many years. Author Shakti Gawain calls it a 'healing crisis.' I like to think of it as a recognition that, on an individual level, only I have the power to change the lens and then zoom in on what I do have in my life and not what I don't. Despite my circumstances – and it's really not easy – a feeling of gratefulness can be chosen. Nobody said it was easy, but this choice is mine.

Gratitude, like so many other things, is a muscle that needs exercising. Crisis and suffering can help to make me grateful, as I come to appreciate in a profound way that I do not have what I took for granted previously. Yet the converse can also be true: gratitude can help me to be more resilient in the face of hardship. Here is David Steindl-Rast again: *day and night gifts keep pelting down on us. If we were aware of this, gratefulness would overwhelm us. But we go through life in a daze. A power failure makes us aware of what a gift electricity is; a sprained ankle lets us appreciate walking as a gift, a sleepless night, sleep. How much we are missing in life by noticing gifts only when we are suddenly deprived of them.*

I often think about these words. What a gift a good night's sleep is. I hope to never again take that for granted. On the nights that I sleep, I can start my day with a prayer of gratitude on my lips and remain in communion with that at stages throughout the day. On those days I haven't slept, there is always something else to celebrate or feel grateful for. Yes, it is harder to access that when I feel so awful. But I can do it. I find it helps to write it down, in a notebook or a journal. I used to write a list of three daily gratitudes at the end of each day in my journal; these days, with one of my 'gold' friends, we have a practice of sending each other three daily gratitudes on WhatsApp. Even on the very hardest of days, I am humbled by these 'day and night gifts' that gleam like Hansel and Gretel's breadcrumbs in the moonlight.

Gratitude isn't the same thing as positive thinking. People would sometimes say things to me like, think positively. Or, if you really believe you will be better, you will be. Or, stop worrying about it and you'll be fine. In 'positive thinking,' sometimes we are not claiming or feeling our experiences or allowing ourselves to be vulnerable. According to Pema Chödrön, *affirmations are like screaming that you're okay in order to overcome this whisper that you're not.* Gratitude is about embracing reality. Isn't it kinder to say *Yes, this is where I am at* and breathe into that space? By connecting with that tender place of reality, we open to the possibility to seeing, in the words of composer Tchaikovsky, who suffered numerous cyclical lapses into depression, that *there are many thorns, but the roses are there too.*

While I am staying in Buttercup Meadow, I take long walks along the clifftops. I prepare simple meals in the motorhome. I buy a bowl of chips and a pint of beer and sit outside a village pub. I read a lot and write in my journal. Most of all, I spend time watching and responding to the show of nature. While I am here, I don't really have a choice but to get outside, unless I want to spend four days cooped up in a tiny box that fits little more than a bed and a cooker.

And being here in nature works wonders for my soul. *Give yourself the gift of silence, of listening,* says Jack Kornfield, Author and Buddhist practitioner. *Go out into the woods, the mountains, walk along a meandering stream or the ever-changing sea. Look closely at a hundred kinds of steady, leading trees. Follow the delicate flight of birds... When you are in difficulty, remember the world beckons to you with a bigger story. It invites you to vastness and freedom.*

The healing properties of spending time in nature has been widely documented across the spectrum, from science to art to spirituality. Harvard biologist E.O. Wilson calls the human connection with nature 'biophilia' – the *rich, natural pleasure that comes from being surrounded by living organisms.* And celebrated 19th Century poet, Walt Whitman, was recovering from a paralytic stroke when he pondered on what remains when the world seems unable to offer us what we need: *nature remains; to bring out from their torpid recesses, the affinities of a man or woman with the open air, the trees, fields, the changes of seasons — the sun by day and the stars of heaven by night.*
So not only is it important for me to spend time outside, to adjust my

The Sky Within Rebecca Stonehill

circadian rhythms to the light patterns of day and night, but it is also vital to spend as much time as possible in the natural world. Of course this is more readily available to some of us than others; I, for instance, live in a city, and need to constantly find ways to move beyond the boundaries of the city limits to where the grass is not paved over. But I am also fortunate enough to have use of my legs, and this is not an option for many. But even if you live in densely urban areas, or have a physical disability which does not allow you to do this, being outside in any capacity will help, in some way, to regain an equilibrium. Nature is there: in the murmuration of starlings that wheel through the dying light above concrete car parks; in the woodlice that scuttle and beneath the crackle of dry bark on a lonely tree. Nature cannot be stopped.

It can be wonderful and nurturing to take a walk with a friend or family member, but I make the time to be in nature alone as well. This helps me to really notice in silence what is happening around me and to fine tune my sensory awareness which engenders, in the words of psychoanalyst Adam Philips, 'fertile solitude.' As a human, I am part of this intricate, interconnected web. The ancient Greeks considered the elemental power of nature as something sacred and even Einstein, whom we so closely consider as being concerned with the intellect, said that if we *look deep into nature...then you will understand everything better.*

Deeply rooted in our evolution as a species, for a vast 99% of our genetic history we've been hunter-gatherers, intimately connected with the natural world. Like anything, it may feel easier to get out there when we are feeling at one with the world. But real change can only happen when we turn to nature when our hearts are clouded with grief. Even if it something very small: the feel of the breeze against our skin; taking in a lungful of fresh air; the crunch of leaves beneath our feet, we are reconnecting and reclaiming our genetic heritage and birth right. And in doing so, we are finding, as TS Eliot calls it, *the still point of the turning world.*

While I am staying at Buttercup Meadow, I also swim in the chilly North Sea to find this still point, and my hands and feet go a strange, mottled, yellowish-purple colour. Wild swimming, particularly over the Covid pandemic lockdown and through the winter months, attracted an increasing number of people. The health benefits have been well documented, from improved mental health to an increase in dopamine (a neurotransmitter that's involved in the reward process) to building the fitness of our stress-response systems. I never expected to jump on that particular bandwagon;

swimming through the summer felt fine, but the winter, when there's frost on the ground and river temperatures barely nudge above 6 degrees Celsius? No thanks. There's also the fact that I have particularly poor circulation and feel the cold more than the average person; I can often be found bundled up in numerous layers even during the warmer months.

But I realise through the ache of my sadness, that I need to find ways to feel alive, really alive. And what better way than to be submerged in water so cold it knocks the breath out of me, allowing me no opportunity to think about anything other than trying to regulate my breath? Cold-water swimming is, in many ways, the perfect exercise in mindfulness. For my first winter swim, I enlist Andy and our middle child to join me. We tiptoe down to the sea's edge in our bathing costumes and woolly hats in December as the waves glow a pearly pink from the setting sun. Holding hands, we roar like banshees and launch ourselves into the water. We really don't stay in for long that first time; it's more for a taste of it. And it's cold, but somehow not as cold as we think it will be. Not far behind us, an inquisitive seal bobs about in the waves, it's sweet, whiskery face peering at us in curiosity. Afterwards, we dry ourselves rapidly, tear our bathing suits from our bodies and quickly put on warm layers before diving into the heated car for hot tea and biscuits. It couldn't be more of a perfect first swim and it's only my hands and feet that feel the cold.

I know that I want to do it again, so I decide to go all-out and invest in a wetsuit, gloves and boots. No messing about; if this is going to be a regular thing, or even semi-regular, I need to be warm enough to want to stay in the water for more than ten seconds. Besides, we live much closer to a number of rivers than we do to the sea, and rivers are notorious for being colder to swim in. The next time we go into the water, ice still grazes the grass that we pad over to get in and what I'm not prepared for this time around, even with my boots, gloves and wetsuit, is the pain that splinters my body when I step into the river. It feels like nothing I have ever experienced and I gasp with the aching shock of it. The good thing about this though, that no matter how frozen the water feels, and no matter how much your head tells you to turn back, by the time you've made the effort to get down there and to get into all the gear, turning back simply isn't an option. It's like a silent pact has been made between you and the river and by this stage, you can't turn back; to do so would spoil the rest of your day.

So, you steady your breathing and you swim. And for those few minutes of splintering cold, so icy it feels as though a layer of your skin is being peeled

The Sky Within Rebecca Stonehill

away, you are a glorious one with the river. Since then, I have swum many times in different locations around Norfolk during the winter months. It is still incredibly cold, but perhaps because my body knows what is coming, the shock of it doesn't punch the air out of me in the manner it once did. And, as I mentioned before, I have to be completely present to the experience: of lowering myself into the water; of making myself breathe long and deep; of moving my arms and legs. For the time I am in the water, anything that feels less than whole evaporates: my grief, my exhaustion, my frustration. And then, as I am swimming, something else happens: as my legs tangle with river weeds and I move aside some overhanging willow that trails onto the water's surface, I start to tune into the generosity of nature's circus. During my river swims, I have seen the flash of a kingfisher plunging into the water, the flap of a heron's wings, the darting of dozens of tiny insects I have no name for and the whirring wings of electric-blue damselflies, fragile as lace. There is, really, nothing like it. I see things that I know I wouldn't see if I were walking on the banks. I feel as though I have entered a secret world of river, earth, sky and wings and, for those minutes, I can be truly part of the soaring melody of nature. I am not a particularly strong swimmer. Nor am I an elegant swimmer. But now I am able to slip soundlessly as an otter into the cold water and once I'm in, I simply swim. The act in itself helps to remind me I am alive and more than that; I am part of something incredible. Marine biologist and author Rachel Carson who was considered to be one of the founders of the global environmental movement so rightly stated that *our origins are of the earth… there is in us a deeply seated response to the natural universe, which is part of our humanity.*

When we are very low, sometimes the last thing we feel able to do is get outside. But we must. The days I have not been true to my inner knowledge of this necessity, I have suffered more. The poet John Keats who penned some of the best-loved poems amongst the Romantics, suffered from crippling depression for many years of his short life. Reflecting upon the grief he often felt, however, he was able to notice that *the setting sun will always set me to rights.*

John Keats knew what so many inherently feel once in natural surroundings: that the frame of our problems gently shifts. There is a sense of a greater unfolding and the quiet, steady heartbeat of the natural world that keeps turning, that keeps doing what it must do no matter what else is going on. I love Mary Oliver's short, powerful poem, *I Go Down To The Shore*, that expresses this so perfectly:
I go down to the shore in the morning

> *and depending on the hour the waves*
> *are rolling in or moving out,*
> *and I say, oh, I am miserable,*
> *what shall –*
> *what should I do? And the sea says*
> *in its lovely voice:*
> *Excuse me, I have work to do.*

Of course it does. The sea has work to do, just as the blackbird does and the newt and the new growth of bluebells that carpet the forest floor. I'm not convinced that anything else has the power and potential to lift us quite like nature. I don't know how many times I have been doubled over with the weight of grief and forced myself outside into the elements. Nature can't take the grief away, but if we stop and look, really notice, something shifts inside us. We are hard-wired for wildness and if we get out there and allow ourselves to be among the shifting patterns of the sky and the wind, the birds that drift overhead and the breeze rippling through long grass, we are answering a primeval call embedded deep within our DNA that our ancestors intuited in a way greatly lost to us. But we can go back to that place and open our hearts to what it can offer up to help and heal us.

During the first lockdown of the Covid pandemic, I took the same walk every day. Just as so many others around the globe also tuned into the wild spaces of their local neighbourhoods, I started to notice the 'weeds' reaching out through cracks in the pavement, the profusion of wildflowers growing out of walls and the flora and fauna of my local urban environment. I found myself looking at an old book on wildflowers that had sat on our bookshelf for years but I had never explored, identifying what I had seen and breathing the names, some of them familiar and others not, like a spell. Then I got an app on my phone so I could also identify them when I was out and about.

Now, on the days when I find grief and depression snapping at my heels, when I force myself out of the house and see something I recognise, the very naming of a wildflower brings me comfort, just like coming into contact with an old friend, and making new friends when I see something I don't know. On a recent walk, as I strode across some marshes alone near where I live, I felt so low that I couldn't bring myself to stop and take in any of the wildflowers. But I had to walk myself into it, and by the time I had internalised the steady rhythm of putting one foot in front of another and allowed myself to be soothed by nature, I could sense the subtle change

The Sky Within Rebecca Stonehill

within. By the time I walked back, I felt lighter. I felt part of the world. And I stopped to look at the wildflowers, my old friends, and I listened to the birdsong. Perhaps that will be the next thing for me. Perhaps one day I will be able to identify different birds from their melodies.

Grateful living in difficult times, writes Kristi Nelson, *can help to build a bridge from despair to empowerment and from grief to engagement. And, importantly, it can keep our hearts open when they want to close.* And now, as I sit on the steps of my motorhome, hot mug of tea at my fingertips, vase of wildflowers beside me and birds diving and darting past in and out of the hedgerow, I feel it settle around me like a second skin: yes. I am truly a part of this world. And I am grateful.

A Lamp to Yourself

'Meditation is a practice that allows us to accept our life moment by moment without judgment or the expectation for life to be other than what it is.'

Douglas Abrams, Author

During my last term of University, I sit at one of the library computers, idly tapping away on the keyboard to bring up a few pages on careers advice. Whilst I am doing this, I notice a piece of paper underneath the desk and reach down to pick it up. I'm about to throw it in the bin, when something catches my eye: somebody has circled a website address for teaching abroad. Curious, I tap the address into the search engine and read about opportunities for young people to go to different countries to teach English. I digest the information, lean back in my chair and narrow my eyes.

Six months later, graduation and various temping jobs to save money behind me, I find myself in a village in Tamil Nadu, India, teaching English in a girls' secondary school. I have never taught anything in my life; nor have I ever been to India. I haven't made this decision to be obtuse or rebellious; I genuinely have no idea what I want to do with my life and I am buying myself time. By rights, I have already had my pre-university gap year, and now that I've spent three years at university, I 'should' be applying for jobs and settling down. I certainly feel the pressure of that – mine is a high-brow university and many of the people I know are already comparing starting salaries for their new graduate positions. But these conversations leave me cold. I've been studying Anthropology for three years and while it's been interesting and fun, the truth is that my heart has never been in it. All I've ever wanted to be is a writer and amidst my scant revision for my third-year final exams, I am spending far more time working on a novella for a friend's 21st birthday. You can't be a writer, I've been told numerous times. Being a writer isn't a job. And while I can attest to the fact that it's not easy to earn a living from writing, what if the desire to write has you in a noose hold and simply refuses to let go? What then?

I think my decision to go to India stems from both a reaction against the tidy

The Sky Within Rebecca Stonehill

tying of bows of post-university jobs, a longing to see more of the world and an innate need to carve my own tracks; to observe, armed with journal and camera. I predict staying for around six months, but I end up not leaving for a year. Whilst in India, as well as teaching English in Tamil Nadu for three months, I travel up and down the country by train and bus, sometimes alone and sometimes with people I meet; I do voluntary work at the Missionaries of Charity in Calcutta, helping look after disabled children, many of whom have been abandoned; I visit temples and learn to eat with my hands so that the metallic clink of cutlery starts feeling strange; I wear *salwar kameez* and learn the best way to tie a *sari*. And, of course, I write my thoughts and impressions down in a huge journal I lug around in my rucksack.

All of this has a huge impact on me and India creeps beneath my skin as stealthily as an approaching dawn. But perhaps the part of this journey across the Indian sub-continent that stays with me the longest is visiting Ladakh, in the far north reaches of India, up beyond the Himalayas and Kashmir. Bordering Tibet, Ladakh doesn't feel like being in India at all. Here, there is none of the cloying heat and the throng of bodies weaving through crowded marketplaces or piling onto trains. Cut off by snow for a large part of the year, Ladakh is sharp, rose and ochre mountain beauty; crystalline air that makes your chest heave with the high altitude and a proud, predominantly Buddhist population who share far more culturally with neighbouring Tibet than they do with India.

Getting to Leh, the region's capital, is not straightforward if you don't have the money to fly there from Delhi. The only other option is to take a bus from Manali, a town in Himachal Pradesh, along the second highest highway in the world. This road reaches a dizzying altitude of 5,328 metres as it travels across winding passes and precipitous hairpin bends. I leave the hostel groggily at four in the morning, bumping into a Dutch traveller I met the day before booking bus tickets. The engine of the only auto-rickshaw we can find isn't working and so, rucksacks on our backs, we push the rickshaw to the top of the hill before jumping in so that it freewheels downwards all the way to the bus station. The mix of nationalities leaving Manali for Leh is staggering: as well as Indians, there are English, Spanish, French, German, Dutch, Portuguese, Polish, Japanese, Italian, Israeli, American and Canadian. I sit next to a Spaniard who doesn't speak much English and at that point, my Spanish isn't up to much so I stare out of the window at the changing landscape as our bus climbs higher. It doesn't take long at all to reach snow level and the higher we climb, the more barren the landscape, the trees and grass disappearing to leave a rocky terrain of browns and greys, flowers and shrubs intermittently pushing through the stones. As we continue, we start to see Tibetan prayer flags fluttering and rocks piled one on top of another.

The first night we spend in a tent encampment, high up on an open, sweeping plateau and overlooking snow-peaked mountains. It is stunningly beautiful but so cold and after a dinner of *dal bhat* at an overpriced, captive-market restaurant and some whisky from the Dutch traveller's hip flask, I go to bed in the tent wearing five layers, double socks, gloves and two sleeping bags. The next day, after having felt relief at not suffering from the altitude sickness so many others are struggling with, I now have a bad headache and feel dehydrated. We drive for another five hours then stop at a roadside camp, assuming it's for a lunch-stop. But a few hours later, we haven't moved anywhere and it's hard to get any information out of anyone. Eventually, we learn that a curfew has been imposed upon Leh due to three monks being killed there and nobody is allowed in and out. All we can do is sit tight and wait to see what happens.

It is a curious scene up here on this frozen mountain plateau at 4,800 metres: a French couple are eating a never-ending supply of baguette and cheese (where on earth did they buy such luxuries?); a Korean lady is vomiting continually from the altitude sickness; an English couple are cleaning up their auto-rickshaw that they have driven here all the way from Kerala, India's southernmost state and a middle-aged Canadian couple are sitting with their bearded and dreadlocked yogi son wearing robes to help him move into a cave where he will apparently meditate. We are going nowhere fast and some people are managing to catch rides back to Manali. I wonder if it is not my fate to reach Ladakh. But after a freezing cold night in a large open-sided tent, I am playing backgammon with a Portuguese girl from the bus when a ripple starts to spread amongst the remaining travellers that we can start moving again. A cheer goes up from the cold, bedraggled crowd and we all clamber back on to the bus, eager to get going. We spend six hours making our way through passport checkpoints, drive over the highest pass and drive by squat, white, rectangular houses. Finally, after what feels like another eternity, we arrive in Leh, still under a curfew following the problems there. I have made it.

I never find out why those monks were tragically killed – information that is not just hearsay is hard to come by – but after the curfew lifts, it is easy to move around the city. During the month I spend in Ladakh (which precedes probably the longest journey of my life: travelling all the way back down

The Sky Within Rebecca Stonehill

to Chennai overland in the south of India to fly back to England), I visit monasteries, meet some wonderful people, take buses out of the city and trek through remote villages. I also do a five-day meditation course because so many people that I've met during this time in India have done one course or another, and I'm curious to know what it's all about. Just like the bus up to Ladakh, there are people taking part from all over the world. On the first couple of days, it's such hard work that I consider packing it in. I find it intensely irritating that a number of people around me can be happy to sit there serenely for such a long time. It's interesting to note from my India diary a 'fear' I have of being on my own and not having something to occupy myself with. *What's so wrong with just being still and quiet?* I ask in the diary. *I've always been so bad at that.*

The meditation challenges me profoundly, and that's what leaves me furious for those first days. I am angry that I am so fidgety; angry that my mind keeps wandering to home and people I have met and places I have been to here in India. I'm not sure it ever gets easier while I am doing the course, but I certainly stop feeling so desperate about not being able to do it 'right.' And I think it's an important lesson for me in many ways and something must resonate, because by the time I am back in England, I find myself setting my alarm half an hour earlier than normal every morning so I can sit and meditate. Just as during the course, I don't find it easy, especially when my bed is so warm and I could be sleeping for longer. But there is something that propels me onwards and encourages me to keep setting that alarm. I'm not entirely sure what it is. Perhaps I am frustrated by this inability to be still and quiet; this need to always be doing in some form or another and something inside recognises that I do need to simply stop sometimes and tune in. I don't know exactly what I'm tuning into, but it doesn't seem to matter.

In my early twenties, sleep isn't an issue for me. Granted, I'm not the heaviest or soundest of sleepers, but if I have a bad night, on the whole I make up for it the following night. Looking back on those years now, my time in India and the experimenting with meditation and mindfulness, I couldn't possibly have known that I was opening a door that would never close again and paving a path for something that would, in my later years, bring me solace and strength again and again. As the years unwind, not only do I stop running from being still and quiet, but I come to welcome it in a way I welcome few other things. I have been interested in different spiritual practices ever since I was young, looking for answers at my school Christian Union and later embracing my Jewish roots and spending time in Israel.

But the only practice that really settles as something to move forwards with is Buddhism; not that I feel a need to 'become' Buddhist but rather that it's a philosophy I can learn from. I don't need to commit myself and I don't need to set anything in stone. I can just practise. And that's exactly what I do when I meditate: I practise.

The spiritual philosophy of Buddhism emerged almost two and a half thousand years ago when a rich young prince from Nepal, Siddharta Gautama, lived in a lavish palace with high walls to protect him from the outside world. But he became increasingly curious about the outside world and asked his charioteer to take him into the town. Siddharta was horrified by the poverty and suffering he witnessed outside the palace walls and realised how shielded his life was. Renouncing his princely status and luxuries, he ventured out into the world with only the clothes on his back, finally arriving at a large tree. He sat meditating beneath this *bodhi* tree for forty-nine days, before sharing what he had learnt about non-violence, compassion, forgiveness and tolerance with five people who travelled around telling others about Siddharta's insights, a man who came to be known as the Buddha. And so began the spiritual practices and beliefs of Buddhism.

The more we meditate or engage with our lives mindfully, the more we can recognise our thoughts for what they are. Buddhist teacher from seven hundred years past, Japanese Zen Master Dōgen, says that *meditation is not a way to enlightenment, nor is it a method of achieving anything at all. It is peace and blessedness itself.* Understanding this truth helps me to take the pressure off myself. By meditating, I am not trying to be spiritual or achieve enlightenment or even anything close to that. It is, quite simply, an act of self-love. It is taking time out for myself. And if I ever feel wistfully nostalgic about those days in my early twenties of travel and buzz and parties and activity, I can also feel compassion for that young woman who didn't know how to be still or how to spend time alone. Now, it feels more important than almost anything else.

There is nothing mystical about meditation. The word itself comes from the same root words from Sanskrit and Greek as medicine and it means 'to take the measure of and to care for.' It is a way of being present, of recognising our drifting thoughts and of returning to the breath over and over. But considerable misconceptions exist about what meditation is and isn't. It is often thought that it is all about 'getting rid' of our thoughts, but in many ways, it is quite the opposite of this. It is impossible to get rid of our thoughts. But it is possible to recognise them when they arise with a non-judgmental attitude, and then allowing the attachment we have to them to recede.

We often worry that our minds jump around far too much to be able to sit for any period of time, just as I did when I was learning in that room high in the mountains of Ladakh. Yet physiologist Herbert Benson says that the 'relaxation response', in other words, the point at which the practice becomes beneficial for us, is by identifying those times during meditation when our mind wanders and bringing it back. That simple response is where the gold lies, in the resolve to gently re-root our minds in the present. The beauty of meditation is that it can help to break the chain of relentless thoughts and soundbites that reverberate through our minds. Author Douglas Abrams words sum it up succinctly for me: *meditation is a practice that allows us to accept our life moment by moment without judgment or the expectation for life to be other than what it is.*

And what of the ancient philosophy of Buddhism? A central focus is making friends with our minds in a similar vein to what I talked about in the third chapter of this book, *The Story of Thoughts*. *Lojong*, a practice from the Tibetan Buddhism tradition, is essentially mind training, the basic notion being to make friends with what we instinctively seek to reject. This means moving closer to the pain, challenging our usual knee-jerk responses and finding that space within us that Chinese Zen master Pai-Chang (720-814) calls our 'Buddha nature'. We don't have to be a certain type of person or adhere to a certain set of beliefs or call ourselves Buddhist to benefit from this. *To realise your true nature*, he says, *you must wait for the right moment and the right conditions. When the time comes, you are awakened as if from a dream. You realise that what you have found is your own and doesn't come from anywhere outside.* I'm not sure there is any time of 'awakening' for me. It certainly doesn't happen during those days of sitting cross-legged in Ladakh. Instead, it is a slow burn that begins in those mountains when I am twenty-one and carries me still today in so many ways. But yes, what I have is my own and mapping my inner landscape is a life's work.

In the midst of a very difficult time, a close friend recommended a book called *How to be Sick* by Toni Bernhard. Within its pages, I discovered for the first time a number of different practices used in the Buddhist tradition which I have woven into the fabric of my own life challenges. Perhaps I was practising some of them anyway without having named them, but it's been invaluable for me to pause and look at each one individually. Toni Bernhard, law professor and Buddhist, was fully immersed in her life, family and career when she fell sick from an incurable fatiguing illness that has left her bed-bound for many years. She has been through all the cycles of hope, crashing disappointment and surrender to the unknown and writing her book was a long, physically painful and often arduous journey. But it was a gift of deep generosity to share her story and practices with others. I urge you to read the book if you are suffering with your health, but even if it isn't health issues you are grappling with, as Sylvia Boorstein rightly points out in the book's foreword, *this book is for all of us. Sooner or later, we are all going to "not get better."*

I'd like to mention a number of the practices that Toni Bernhard outlines in her book; these have all been sources of comfort for me during difficult times. The first is *Khanti*, described as 'patient endurance,' an active and often difficult but vital practice. Keeping patient endurance at my side when I am having a hard time is an act of deep self-compassion for myself. But how do I cultivate *khanti*, especially when I am in the midst of acute distress? The first step is to accept that suffering (*dukkha*) is part and parcel of the tapestry of life. Stress and difficulties are bound to visit, and to wound me. At the same time, suffering is temporary. Nothing lasts for ever, and in acknowledging this, a recognition may be able to open up that I have spent a great deal of time and energy in trying to avoid *dukkha*.

Khanti speaks of accepting uncertainty and knowing that I may not have all the answers and quite possibly, never will. The 'not-knowing' can bring with it deep-rooted fear and insecurity. But I try to think of it as an open-ended question, or in the Zen tradition, the 'emptying of our cup.' Imagine this: a cup filled to the brim with all my certainties and ideas about how my life should look and who I am and who other people are being slowly emptied out until it sits there, an empty vessel entirely free from the stories and answers I try to make myself feel more secure with. Ultimately, I know that this clash between reality not aligning with expectations can bring me great pain.

Metta is another practice whereby loving kindness is directed both towards myself and towards others. According to Toni Bernhard, *to a sick body, a troubled mind, or a hardened heart, nothing is more soothing than metta practice*. I know I am not the only one to be incredibly hard on myself, the inner judge and critic distorting the beauty that lies within. I know I would never dream of treating my closest friends the way I sometimes treat myself, but somehow, because it's just 'me', I let it go. And so the barrage of remorseless self-judgment continues.

The Sky Within Rebecca Stonehill

I like to think of a *metta* practice as a series of concentric, ever-widening circles with myself at the centre, the heart of the circle. I find a phrase or a few phrases that work for me. Here are a few that are easy to remember: May I be peaceful, May I be free from suffering, May I be well. I repeat these phrases a number of times, saying them slowly and staving off the temptation to rush through them; really listening to the words as I say them (out loud or in my head) and hear their timbre and resonance. I try to allow myself to really sink into what these phrases are expressing.

To be free from suffering is not putting the request out there for my suffering to stop, because as has been proven time and again, the more I try to fight what afflicts me, the less likely it is to diminish. Rather, it is about the release of suffering of the mind, which often torments me more than what is happening itself. Once I have directed those phrases towards myself, the next step is calling to mind somebody very dear to me. I go through the same steps, but exchanging 'I' for 'you.' The third step is to go through the same process with a person I don't know well, for example the man at the check-out counter at the supermarket this morning or the Big Issue vendor who sells his magazine near the market square. Finally, I extend the practice to somebody that I find difficult in my life; perhaps a person who 'triggers' or aggravates me. As with all of these stages, I simply notice what comes up for me and how these thoughts are impacting on my mind, body and emotions. Anna Black, Mindfulness Teacher, says that *our body is a true barometer of our feelings*, so it is useful to keep checking in with how this metta practice is affecting me on a physical level. I don't have to keep the same set of phrases as I progress with the practice: it feels important to allow myself to be fluid and adapt them as I feel works. *What makes metta such a different approach*, says Pema Chödrön, *is that we are not trying to solve a problem. We are not striving to make pain go away or to become a better person. In fact, we are giving up control and letting concepts and ideals fall apart.*

Moving on, *mudita* means sympathetic joy. This is essentially cultivating happiness in the joy of others and is particularly relevant when presented with chronic sickness and an inability to live our lives as we once did. But even if we are not talking of a debilitating illness, *mudita* can offer a gentle beauty. I have found envy to be such a natural, knee-jerk reaction to watching what I believe to be others playing out their lives in the way I would like to myself. *I wish I could still do that*; these words can feel emblazoned on to a great banner across the sky.

This is a difficult practice, but one that I have experimented with and will continue to do so. Even though it may feel like I am faking it at first, trying to engender that joy for others when it feels anything but real, it's important I remain with it. As Toni Bernhard says, *sticking with a practice even though it may feel artificial or fake allows that practice to enter our hearts, our minds, and our bodies.* Envy can be crippling to our mental well-being; Douglas Abrams describes it as 'a poison tinged with guilt and self-criticism.' But to cultivate *mudita*, much like *metta*, it's important that I first soften into an awareness of what is taking place in my own body and mind and meeting whatever I find there with compassion. From this point, I can start to practice sympathetic joy for others in my life. It's a recognition of our shared humanity and I say to mysel, *I'm happy that you are happy*, letting it roll gently through my mind like moving waves without fixating on it. Other phrases to play around with are:

May your happiness last.
May your happiness grow.
May your happiness and good fortune radiate.

Sometimes, I also take it to the next step in a similar way to *metta*, thinking of a beloved person, a neutral person and a difficult person.

The next concept is *annica* which looks at the idea of everything being impermanent, or that anything can happen at any time. Things are changing, all the time, and no one moment is the same as the next. The sky, for example, is always changing with clouds, sun, wind and rain passing through. My own experience is no different, and just as different weather patterns blow through, so do my thoughts and associated moods. The wise and self-compassionate path is knowing, understanding and accepting impermanence and uncertainty. Not being able to feel this stable ground beneath my feet can be deeply unsettling, but by letting go of this I can open to a spaciousness that can be mine whenever I call upon it.

Finally, *upekkha* means equanimity. It is a mental calmness and evenness of temper, especially in difficult situations, which is what makes it so relevant during difficult times. Toni Bernhard describes equanimity as *accepting life as it comes to us without blaming anything or anyone – including ourselves.* It's not a simple practice to take on board, because it may feel (and also be viewed this way by others) that I am being passive or indifferent or lacking the passion to make positive change in my life. I found this on my journey, that as I tried to practise equanimity in the face of suffering, others would sometimes urge me to be 'more active' in my search to cure myself. But cultivating *upekkha* takes great practice and courage; ultimately, using tools of meditation, our

The Sky Within Rebecca Stonehill

levels of mental suffering can decrease and a gentle equanimity increase.

Be a lamp to yourself, Siddharta said. *Be your own confidence. Hold to the truth within yourself, as to the only truth.* Something about these words resonates deeply when I am learning to meditate. They tell me that I don't need anything from outside myself to find self-esteem and confidence; that my truth and everything I need to live a meaningful life is within. For somebody who has spent the first two decades of her life seeking meaning and worth solely from external stimuli, friendships and experiences, this is a revelation. Fast forward more than two further decades and checking in, whether it is for meditation practice or moments of mindfulness, has carried me through some of my hardest times. It's hard to imagine what my life would look like without it today; how I would move through those times of anxiety or panic or the clamour of my mind that hurls a steady barrage of untruths at myself.

His Holiness the Dalai Lama is masterful at demystifying something that is traditionally thought of as belonging to a spiritual elite: *in my own practice I engage mostly in… a form of mental investigation where you can see your thoughts as thoughts and learn not to be chained to them, not to identify with them. You come to recognise that your thoughts do not necessarily reflect the truth.*

Learning to be with ourselves, and how to meditate or engage in mindful practice is a life's work. But it doesn't have to be all or nothing. Anything we do to check in with ourselves, no matter how small, is sewing a seed that one day we may be able to weave and harvest into something that nurtures and fills us.

The End of the Story

'Most people try to hold on to the thing that is no longer part of their lives, and they stop themselves in their lives in that way. I have come to see loss as a stage in a process. It's not the bottom line. It's not the end of the story. What happens next is very, very important.'

Rachel Naomi Remen

This isn't really the end of the story; in fact, it's only the beginning.

Taking up my telescope now, I view myself as a younger woman sitting on a clifftop on Wasini Island, not sure if I have the strength to continue. The note I read from my eldest daughter to Father Christmas, the earnest wish of a child to bring peace to her mother in some undefinable way, opened up in me that night a torrent of such grief that I felt it were literally cleaving my soul from my body, almost like those daemons of Philip Pullman's in *His Dark Materials*: if they are removed, the person can literally not survive.

There is a magazine in the UK called *The Big Issue*, sold by homeless and vulnerably housed men and women. I have always bought the *Big Issue* and particularly enjoy reading the double page spread each week entitled 'Letter to my Younger Self.' They are generally writing to themselves as a teenager, but I love the premise of it, no matter the age. If I were to write a letter now to my younger self in Wasini Island; to that self seated in the A&E unit; to that woman who endlessly traipsed the streets of London sobbing while her daughter went to the Harry Potter play, I'd tell her yes, you do have the strength to continue and that it cannot be any other way. You do, because you have people whom you love. And because you are loved.

In April 2015, the Archbishop Desmond Tutu travelled to the Dharamshala in India to help his friend the Dalai Lama celebrate his 80th birthday. During their week together punctuated with tears and laughter, a series of conversations emerged in which they shared their ideas on how to live

The Sky Within Rebecca Stonehill

meaningful lives amidst turmoil, culminating in a book entitled *The Book of Joy*, written by Douglas Abrams. It's almost impossible to distil that week's wisdom into a sentence, but if I had to choose something, it would be the Archbishop's insistence that although sadness on the surface may seem like the most direct challenge to joy, it often leads us directly to empathy, compassion and a recognition of our great need for connection. That speaks such volumes to me. And if we can catch even a single thread of its truth and weave it into our being, we are one step closer to understanding the beautiful dichotomy of the role of suffering in our lives.

I described earlier my journey to Ladakh in the far north of India at the age of twenty-one. But this isn't the only time I travel to Ladakh. The second is when my family and I leave Kenya and decide to spend six months backpacking around India before returning to the UK. There are many times during the course of these six months when I don't think I can do this trip anymore; that I am exhausted to the depth of my being from lack of sleep and I just need to stop. To go back to England early. But one thing that keeps me going is our plan to go to Ladakh. I am desperate to return, twenty years later, and see what Andy and our children make of the stark beauty of this mountainous, Buddhist region. Of course Leh and the surrounding villages have changed a great deal in the intervening years, but I still fall in love with it, all over again. On one of our last days there (again, just before embarking on the trip back to England – though I cannot deny that this time we flew between Delhi and Leh and back again), we hear rumours that His Holiness the Dalai Lama will be visiting his summer residence which is located outside Leh. I have always wanted to see the Dalai Lama. Always. I am profoundly moved by something he carries within him – an acceptance of what is. He and his people have endured so much: losing a homeland and the ongoing persecution of Tibetan culture, language and its very existence. And yet, through all of this, he is filled with humility, grace, a profound appreciation for life and an endearing sense of humour.

I know that I have to see him, and after the rumours are confirmed, the five of us rise early and take a bus out to Choglomsar where we join the throngs lining the roads up to his summer residence. The vast majority are Buddhist devotees, many of them Tibetan refugees who fled persecution in Tibet for a landscape that is not dissimilar to their homeland. People are waving Tibetan flags and clutching prayer beads and chanting mantras. The atmosphere is electric and it begins to build as the Dalai Lama's advance party drive ahead in open-top vehicles in traditional Ladakhi clothes as the crowds lining the street cheer. I have taken so many photos during our time in India but this time, I cannot lift my camera up in case I miss him; I cannot risk it, nor do I want to. For I sense that what I am about to witness will be a once-in-a-lifetime gift.

After what feels like hours of waiting, the Dalai Lama is driven past slowly in his car. For security reasons, he cannot be in an open-top vehicle like the others in his accompanying party. But there is no mistaking him and he is so close, I want to reach out and touch the pane of glass that separates us. He is smiling broadly, that joyful smile that characterises him, and his hands are together in a prayer position as he bows and smiles to the crowd, again and again. Instinctively, my hands come together as I also bow and smile, looking straight at him and he looks – at least, to me, it feels this way – straight at me.

And then, I do something I am not expecting. I burst into tears. This story has been imbued with the stuff of legend in my family. Oh, that time in Ladakh when Mama saw the Dalai Lama and started crying! One or other of my children occasionally mirthfully recount this tale to friends. I don't say anything, but I smile at the memory of it. What was it that made me cry upon seeing him? I've thought about it a lot since. At a fundamental level, he is somebody who has known suffering, and looking at him that day, I know that he recognises that in other people, yet he sees the whole person. Despite the fleeting nature of it, when he passes by I feel whole, even in my brokenness.

And yet, we all suffer, each and every one of us. So why do I have this extreme reaction to his presence? If I fine tune it, perhaps it is that he lives his belief that we are unable to make peace with the outer world unless we make peace with ourselves. And this, I know, is something I have been seeking for many years: to deeply love and accept myself, no matter what I am going through. *I find hope in the darkest of days,* he has said, *and focus in the brightest. I do not judge the universe.* He is so right; it's been tempting to view my experiences through over the years with a lens of injustice. I don't want to live this way... I didn't ask for this. No, I did not. But this is what the universe has given me, so what if I change the lens to a wide-angle? To see what I can learn from it?

I spend a lot of time writing down inspiring quotes; I have a notebook specially dedicated to the things people have said and written that stir something in me or make me think and I often put them on post-it notes and stick them in strategic places where I'm likely to keep reading them.

The Sky Within Rebecca Stonehill

But a close friend once suggested that I don't just rely on the words of other people, but also find my own mantra; something that works uniquely for me.

How right she was. I thought about it and came up with *one day at a time*. And yet, I was having such a rough time that this mantra felt too big. I couldn't even look at a picture as big as twenty-four hours. So I changed it, to *one breath at a time*. And I thought, Yes, I can do that. Yes.

I am an introvert. I cannot stand on a pedestal to shout out to people what I am going through and I cannot use my social media platform to reach others because this doesn't feel like my natural space. But here's what I can do: I can write these words and hope to reach people this way. Writing this book has been a reminder to myself to live the practices I have been speaking of, to show compassion towards myself. I really do believe that's the most important step we can take on our individual journeys of suffering: to be kind to ourselves. Or more than kind: to be compassionate to the parts of ourselves that are bruised and hurting. Imagine holding a small child who is racked with sobs. How would you be with this child? Tender. Infinitely gentle and compassionate. This is the kind of tenderness we must extend to ourselves.

Of course, this can feel so abstract. But this is why we must begin small, and any step of self-compassion, presence and self-acceptance that we take is strengthening the pathway back to ourselves. Tara Brach says that *we can't really love unconditionally until we accept the life that's here*. Accepting the life that's here doesn't mean that things can't change. Things will change and believing in the impermanence of everything, the *annica*, is a vital heartbeat of being human. Accepting the life that's here means being present to what is going on for myself; giving it space to breathe rather than denying it. It is a constant work and takes great courage, but I do believe that the transformative alchemy of resting in this space can be nothing short of life-changing. I already have the tools inside of me; we all do, though they can feel buried beneath layers of grief. *Life is full of losses and disappointments*, says Rachel Naomi Remen, *and the art of living is to make of them something that can nourish others*. There is mystery at the heart of what we are going through, and we cannot know what the outcome of our suffering will be. The 'not knowing' is painful, particularly when there are no guarantees that one day this will all be behind us. *At the core of hope is a leap of faith*, says Rabbi David Cooper, *not that it will all come out right, but a faith that holds that what we do matters. How it will come to matter, who it will come to inspire, what positive effect it will have – is not ours to know.*'

Poet Rainer Maria Rilke's words are also resonant: '*...if a sadness rises up before you larger than any you have ever seen; if a restiveness, like light and cloud-shadows, passes over your hands and over all you do. You must think that something is happening with you, that life has not forgotten you, that it holds you in its hand; it will not let you fall. Why do you want to shut out of your life any agitation, any pain, any melancholy, since you really do not know what these states are working upon you?*

Even with these tools in place, it takes tremendous courage and wisdom to take this step. It also takes the healing hands of self-compassion and community to set in place the building blocks of lasting inner change. Think of the words of Francis Weller, who has tuned into the nuances of grief, turning it inside out and excavating it for its hidden potency: *every one of us must undertake an apprenticeship with sorrow. We must learn the art and craft of grief, discover the profound ways it ripens and deepens us.*

Try closing your eyes and asking yourself: What is my own personal mantra that can help me with what I am going through? Now put it on post-it notes around the house, write it in your journal or whisper it to yourself throughout the day. You can do this. You can. *Just keep coming home to yourself,* Byron Katie says. *You are the one you've been waiting for.*

Poet Walt Whitman was on intimate terms with depression when he wrote the following words in his seminal poem *A Song of Myself*:

The pleasures of heaven are with me and the pains of hell are with me,
the first I graft and increase upon myself,
the latter I translate into a new tongue.

You too can translate, in some way, what you are going through into a new tongue. What will this look like? How will it mould and change your life and ultimately the lives of others? On your journey, I wish you courage, compassion and community. But, above all else, I wish that you find within yourself that small, bright flame that is always burning, that never goes out.

It is waiting for you.

The Sky Within Rebecca Stonehill

The Sky Within Rebecca Stonehill

Acknowledgements

There are so many people without whom this book would not have been possible.

A heartfelt thank you to Sarah Dudgeon and Max Livingstone-Learmonth for championing this book right from the start – for encouraging me to dig deep and go the extra mile. Also for your brilliant and insightful suggestions and Sarah, your beautiful illustrations that appear with each chapter heading.

Sue Sofroniou and Jeni Neill for reading early versions and for your encouragement.

Rachael Adams for your wonderful book design and Klaudia Wosik for your gorgeous illustrations.

Jasmin Abdel-Moneim, Karen Friedman and Cat Meakin for reading through particular early sections and helping me to see what needed to stay and what needed to go.

My sister Louisa Burns, mother Liz Jacques, stepfather Peter Jacques and parents-in-law, Liz and Mike Narracott for your patience, love and unfailing support.

My 'gold' friends, Tamzin Pinkerton, Maria Schlesinger and Réne Petersen, deep gratitude for your presence, warmth and wisdom and for always meeting me exactly where I'm at.

Alex Elite-Marcandonatou for reading a later version, providing invaluable feedback and for becoming such an enriching, significant soul in my life. Thank you also for your endorsement which graces the cover of this book.

My new Norfolk community who have helped endlessly for me to root myself in this land and provided me with so much love and joy: Cata

Parrish, Chloe Yates, Mae-ling Yeung & Lucy Puttock.

Gretchen Heffernan for your incredible support and belief in this book when so many others said it would be impossible to market and that I'm not an 'expert' in the field (!)

Catherine Moore from Moore & Moore Living, for finally finding a therapist who 'gets' me.

Sarah McConnell from Consera Relationship Wellness for the support you have provided to Andy and myself as a couple, for your presence and ability to coax out the conversations that need to happen.

And last, but not least, the four precious souls to whom this book is dedicated: Andy, Maya, Lily and Benji. I love you profoundly.

Resources and Further Reading

Please find below a list of wise and wonderful people that I have mentioned in the book, some of them a number of times and others only in passing. But all of them are more than worthy of further exploration.

Tara Brach
'What would it be like if I could accept life – accept this moment – exactly as it is?'

Clinical psychologist, psychotherapist and meditation teacher Tara Brach has probably featured most consistently of all the practitioners I have turned to over the years. Blending Western psychology with Buddhist practice she gently and masterfully draws us to mindfully nurture our inner lives and, in so doing, to engage fully and compassionately with the world around us.

As well as having written a number of books (for example *Radical Acceptance* and *Radical Compassion*), she also has a podcast where she shares meditations and reflections and a YouTube Channel.

tarabrach.com

Francis Weller
'It was through the dark waters of grief that I came to touch my unlived life… There is some strange intimacy between grief and aliveness, some sacred exchange between what seems unbearable and what is most exquisitely alive.'

Francis Weller is a psychotherapist, writer and soul activist. His book, *The Wild Edge of Sorrow*, has touched me in way that few others have and it has become a staple work that I re-read each year. Blending and integrating various traditions from anthropology to indigenous cultures to poetry, Weller uses the healing power of ritual to help people move through deep emotional territories.

francisweller.net

The Sky Within Rebecca Stonehill

Elaine Aron

'Make good boundaries your goal. They are your right, your responsibility, your greatest source of dignity.'

Dr Elaine Aron was the first person to research and write about the innate trait of high sensitivity in 1991, spearheading an area of study that has since grown exponentially. Aron's pioneering book, *The Highly Sensitive Person – How to thrive when the world overwhelms you*, has sold over a million copies worldwide and been translated into 17 languages. That being said, it still comes as a great surprise to me that high sensitivity is not better understood and, as I mentioned in the book, that more people working in education and healthcare are not conversant in its nuances. How many children out there are labelled as 'difficult' when they are, in fact, simply overwhelmed? And how many people are put on anti-depressants when, actually, what they need is to better understand their temperament and how to manage it?

If you think that you or someone you are close to may identify with this trait, try taking the self-test on the website. I cannot stress enough how important is has been to learn this about myself and while it can be really challenging, if we learn how to manage this trait effectively, it can also become our superpower.

hsperson.com

Toni Bernhard

'Behind every stressful thought is the desire for things to be other than they are.'

As I mentioned in the *Lamp to Yourself* chapter, Toni Bernhard was an active law professor before she was struck with an acute viral affection that impacted every aspect of her life. Her book *How to Be Sick – A Buddhist-inspired guide for the chronically ill and their caregivers* has been of great help to me. She has also written other books and you don't have to be Buddhist to benefit from her words. Although I wouldn't say that I was chronically ill – more chronically sleep-deprived and anguished – this wise guide written by somebody who has been through every emotion related to sickness that we can imagine, provides vital wisdom for moving through suffering, both physical and emotional.

tonibernhard.com

Byron Katie

'*I am a lover of what is, not because I'm a spiritual person, but because it hurts when I argue with reality.*'

Byron Katie has a huge global following that has grown around her powerful inquiry process of doing what is known as 'The Work'. She has written a number of books, runs events, has a YouTube channel and podcast and provides numerous worksheets to help people question the truth of their thoughts.

Her website is a treasure trove and it may be worth watching a video or two of Byron Katie herself going through the Inquiry process with individuals to get a feel for what it's about, before diving in yourself.

thework.com

Pema Chödrön

'*The experiences of your life are trying to tell you something about yourself. Don't cop out on that. Don't run away and hide under your cover. Lean into it.*'

Pema Chödrön is a Buddhist nun who has been writing, teaching and bringing Buddhist philosophy to Western audiences for many years. She has written many books on how to engage compassionately with ourselves and within our communities but the one that I have found most helpful is *When Things Fall Apart*. You will also find several videos and audios on her website.

pemachodronfoundation.org

Etty Hillesum

'*Ultimately, we have just one moral duty: to reclaim large areas of peace in ourselves, more and more peace, and to reflect it toward others. And the more peace there is in us, the more peace there will also be in our troubled world.*'

To my mind, Etty Hillesum is the Anne Frank that nobody has heard of. I would love for her diaries and letters to be more widely read. My hope is that one day Etty Hillesum will be a household name in much the same way as that of her young Jewish neighbour who sat in an attic on the other side of Amsterdam, pouring her dreams and frustrations onto paper. Her words, which have taught me a great deal about the nature of gratitude, compassion and true freedom, became so important to me that I chose to use some of them as the title for this book: '*The sky within me is as wide as the one stretching above my head.'*

Edited by Eva Hoffman and published in 1999 by Persephone Books, *An Interrupted Life: The Diaries and Letters of Etty Hillesum 1941-43*, is a must read.

gratefulness.org/resource/etty-hillesum

Anne Lamott
'Hope begins in the dark ... if you just show up and try to do the right thing, the dawn will come. You wait and watch and work: you don't give up.'

Anne Lamott is a writer, teacher and activist. Through her trademark self-deprecating humour and open-hearted honesty, she has become a beloved writer to thousands the world over. Topics often navigated in her writing include her former battle with alcoholism, faith, single parenthood and losing loved ones to cancer. If you'd like to dip into her writing, a good place to start may be *Stitches: A Handbook on Meaning, Hope and Repair*.

You can find Anne Lamott on Facebook.

Brother David Steindl-Rast
'Joy is that kind of happiness that does not depend on what happens.'

David Steindl-Rast is a Benedictine monk who works extensively with interfaith dialogue. He founded the worldwide *Network for Grateful Living* through an interactive website that connects thousands of daily participants from around the globe. This same website provides numerous tools and resources to help us weave the power of gratitude into our lives as well as eCourses, explorations of poetry and reflections.

gratefulness.org

Anthony Ray Hinton
'Pain and tragedy and injustice happen - they happen to us all. I'd like to believe it's what you choose to do after such an experience that matters the most - that truly changes your life forever.'

Reading Anthony Ray Hinton's book, *The Sun Does Shine*, had a similar impact on me to reading Etty Hillesum's diary and letters. I found it profoundly moving, not only the sustained and profound injustice he suffered, but also how he managed so gracefully to navigate a path through his terrible situation to reach out to others. I urge you to read it.

To learn more about Hinton's case and thirty years spent on Death Row, read the following report from the Equal Justice Initiative:

eji.org/cases/anthony-ray-hinton

Brené Brown
'You're imperfect and you're wired for struggle, but you are worthy of love and belonging.'

Brené Brown is a celebrated author, research professor and podcast host who has spent over two decades studying courage, vulnerability, shame and empathy. She has written numerous books (*Daring Greatly* or *Braving the Wilderness* are a good place to start) and her TED talk, *The Power of Vulnerability*, has resonated with hundreds of thousands of viewers. She also hosts two podcasts and provides a number of downloadable resources on her website for work, parenting, the classroom and the challenges of daily life.

brenebrown.com

Elizabeth Gilbert
'I think curiosity is our friend that teaches us how to become ourselves. And it's a very gentle friend and a very forgiving friend, and a very constant one.'

Whilst best known for her 2006 memoir *Eat, Pray, Love*, Elizabeth Gilbert has so many more strings to her bow. In 2015 her book *Big Magic: Creative Living Beyond Fear* was published, helping readers to connect with a joyful spirit of adventure, curiosity and permission. Her fiercely honest and open-hearted missives on Instagram, including the book club she runs (#OnwardBookClub), sharing some inspirational reads, has brought her many more global fans.

elizabethgilbert.com

Maria Popova
'Our undoing always serves an invitation to learn new modes of making: making beauty, making meaning, making the life we want to love and the world we want to live in.'

I can't remember how many years ago I started reading Bulgarian-born Maria Popova's weekly blog, *Brain Pickings*, but ever since I started, it has remained firmly in my browser. Her intelligent and thoughtful articles that range from art to philosophy to poetry to history and everything in between provide a perfect diving board for curious and rewarding living.

Popova started her writings back in 2006 as a weekly email to seven friends. It has since grown into a platform that attracts millions of global readers and has become a poetic, spiritual, creative and intellectual archive.

brainpickings.org

Rachel Naomi Remen

'*Our own wounds make us gentle with the wounds of others and able to trust the mystery of healing, not as a theory but from lived experience.*'

Rachel Naomi Remen is an author, clinical professor and integrative medicine teacher. I first discovered her through listening to her talking to Krista Tippett on her *On Being* podcast in a conversation entitled *The Difference being Curing and Healing*, which I found infinitely wise and reassuring.

Remen wishes to bring about a gentle revolution amongst health practitioners and individuals whereby people can heal by their wholeness, by their very humanity, a very different notion from that of being 'cured.' Her groundbreaking curriculum for medical students, *The Healer's Art*, seeks to restore heart and soul to contemporary medicine. Her books include *Kitchen Table Wisdom* and *My Grandfather's Blessings*.

rachelremen.com

David Whyte

'*Enough.*
These few words are enough
If not these few words, this breath
If not this breath, this sitting here
This opening to the life we have refused again and again
Until now
Until now.'

David Whyte is a renowned poet and essayist whose genre-crossing work pours radiant light upon the fierce, radical beauty of human experience. As well as leading poetry and walking tours in his native Ireland, he writes, teaches and speaks prolifically. To explore his words, try *Consolations: The*

Solace, Nourishment and Underlying Meaning of Everyday Words for prose and *River Flow: New and Selected Poems* for poetry.

davidwhyte.com

Jack Kornfield

'Your suffering is not the end of the story. It doesn't have to define you.'

Jack Kornfield was one of the first teachers to introduce Buddhist mindfulness practice to the West after training as a monk in India, Thailand and Burma. A prolific author, speaker and activist, he provides many resources on his website on Buddhism, anti-racism and dealing with the fall-out from the Covid pandemic. Kornfield also hosts a podcast, *Heart Wisdom*, which shines a light on freeing ourselves from self-judgment and unhappiness.

jackkornfield.com

Mary Oliver

'Someone I loved once gave me
a box full of darkness.
It took me years to understand
that this, too, was a gift.'

Mary Oliver was an award-winning poet who outsold any other in her native United States. The neglect she was subjected to as a child and difficult home life drove her out to the woods and wild landscapes around her home where she started to hone her craft. Her poems and essays touch upon themes of nature, the human spirit and the mystery of our daily experience. So many of her poems have spoken to me over the years, but if you are new to the wonder of Oliver, I'd suggest you begin with *Wild Geese, The Summer Day* and *Praying*.

Mary Oliver died in 2019.

maryoliver.com

Helplines

There are many helplines available for when you are feeling very low with empathic, trained people to listen to you. Here in the UK you can call the

The Sky Within Rebecca Stonehill

Samaritans for free, any time, on 116 123 or CALM (Campaign Against Living Miserably) on 0800 58 58 58 from 5pm–midnight every day.

Elsewhere, a quick online search will bring up local helpline services.

Don't be alone.

www.ingramcontent.com/pod-product-compliance
Lightning Source LLC
Chambersburg PA
CBHW012005090526
44590CB00026B/3888